THE BLESSINGS OF REJECTION

KEYS TO SURVIVING AND ENJOYING THE JOURNEY

VAN SHARPE

PRESS

Cover Design by
Photograph of the author by Solomon's Photography
(252) 641-0054

E-mail: asolomon@suddenlink.net
Dr. Van I. Sharpe
Newness of Life Christian Center
936 Albemarle Avenue
P.O. Box 1462
Tarboro, N.C. 27886
(252) 641-0098
Fax: (252) 823-7110
E-mail: reesiesharpe@embarqmail.com

www.xulonpress.com

In memory of my father,
Eddie Frank Sharpe, who perceived my destiny
before I even had a clue.

ABOUT THE AUTHOR

D r. Van I. Sharpe is a resident and native of Tarboro, N.C. He is a graduate from Tarboro High School in Tarboro and graduated Magna Cum Laude with a B.A. degree in Mass Communications from Shaw University in Raleigh N.C. While attending Shaw University, Dr. Van I. Sharpe was an honor student and a member of various honor societies including: Who's Who Among College Students, Alpha Chi National Honor Society, Alpha Epsilon Rho Honor Society, and National Deans List. He is married to Resunester Sharpe and they are the proud parents of one lovely daughter, Vanneika Aireesh Sharpe.

Dr. Van I. Sharpe is the pastor and founder of Newness of Life Christian Center in Tarboro, N.C. His ministry includes pastoring, flowing in the prophetic, and evangelizing in various states.

CONTENTS

ACKNOWLEDGMENTS

This work would have never been completed without the collaborative effort and support of many special men and women in my life. I am always cognizant of the contributions and impact you've made in my journey towards my ultimate destiny.

My gratitude to my Lord Jesus Christ, who enabled me to write and finish this manuscript. You are the author and the finisher of my faith. I am totally nothing without you.

Thank you Resunester Sharpe, my lovely wife, for your unwavering love and support. Your enthusiasm and labor in the kingdom of God makes my assignment much easier.

Thank you Vanneika Sharpe, my precious daughter, for being sensitive to what your dad has to do as a pastor leading a flock and overseeing other pastors.

Thank you to Martia R. Sharpe, my dear niece, who labored with a smile to help this book be completed. Your comments, insights, and proofreading skills were so helpful. You never cease to amaze Uncle Van!

Thank you Newness of Life Christian Center Family for your diligent love and support. Your compassion and prayers made this vision a reality.

Thank you Deacon Anthony Solomon for your photography work on this book. Your photographic genius at Solomon's Photography never ceases to amaze me.

Thank you Pastors In Covenant (PIC), for always being there with the right word at the right time. Pastors like you and your wives are very hard to find.

Thank you Pastors of the Gathering of Believers, for your prayers and wisdom. You have shown that racial barriers can fall if we really want them to.

Thank you Bishop Marvin Smith for showing me how to never ever quit. The words you poured into my spirit are still bearing fruit in my life today.

Thank you to my brother and two sisters (Pastor Wayne, Pastor Susan and Gloria), who are indeed a source of strength and hope. My gratitude also, goes to my special sister in law, Marjorie, who has always been wonderful.

Last but not least a special thanks to Shirley Sharpe, my mother, who has always been in my corner. Thank you for believing and instilling in me an attitude of confidence through your care.

INTRODUCTION

M ost of the time what I need is not truly the issue. But the real issue seems to be where I've got to go to get what I really need. Or who I have to confront to get what I really need seems to be the most intimidating thing. Yet, the God we serve hides what we need in some strange places. This is so those who are not really hungry want get it. Only those who are desperate in their spirit to embrace what God has purposed to fulfill in their lives are trying to discern where God has hidden their blessings. Jesus disciples were desperate to pay their taxes, so Jesus told them to go look in the fish mouth for the piece of money that met their need.

Samson had to discern that the honey he so desperately needed was in the mouth of a lion. His mother and father never knew where he got the food from, nor did he tell them.

> Judges 14:6,8,9 *"And the Spirit of the Lord came mightily upon him, and he rent him as he would have rent a kid, and he had nothing in his hand: but he told not his father or his mother what he had done. And after a time he returned to take her, and he turned aside to see the carcase of the lion: and*

*behold, there was a swarm of bees and honey in
the carcase of the lion. And he took thereof in his
hands, and went on eating, and came to his father
and mother, and he gave them, and they did eat: but
he told not them that he had taken the honey out of
the carcase of the lion."*

This is where most of the things we really need are. They are inside a lion. There will be some things that will roar up against us. Most of us want our blessings, but we don't want to face a lion. Especially not the lion of "rejection." However, we need to notice based on the previous scripture the lion was no match for Samson once the Spirit of God came upon him. Samson ripped him up like he was nothing. The only thing Samson had to face was the swarm of bees that were buzzing around the dead carcase.

The Spirit of the Lord is moving mightily upon us to rip the lion open. He will make our task simple. Notice Samson had nothing in his hands. This is telling us that it will not be done by our own might and power, but by God's Spirit. All we have to do is scare away the bees and eat the good stuff left inside of the carcase.

Zechariah 4:6 *"...Not by might, nor by power, but
by my spirit, saith the Lord of hosts."*

The Amplified says, *"...Not by might, nor by power,
but by My Spirit [of Whom the oil is a symbol], says
the Lord of hosts."*

Samson never told his parents because he knew they wouldn't like the place where he got the food. Many times we have mighty men and women of God who are refusing to tell us where they've gathered the food. The parents never inquired of Samson where it came from. If they knew, they like many of us would have said, "I'm not eating anything out of a dead lion." Also, his parents would have been wondering where did he get such awesome strength. But God knew it was important for us to know that's why it is penned.

The rejections of life will give you enough to eat and share with those you love. When rejection roars at you, God's Spirit will change you instantly to a man or woman of supernatural power. The power of God that you will begin to demonstrate will turn things around for your neighborhood and family. Go and release the power of the Almighty God!

Acts 1:8 *"But ye shall receive power, after that the Holy Ghost is come upon you: and ye shall be witnesses unto me both in Jerusalem, and in all Judea, and in Samaria, and unto the uttermost part of the earth."*

The Amplified says, *"But ye shall receive power (ability, efficiency, and might)..."*

The Living Bible says, *"But when the Holy Spirit has come upon you, you will receive power to testify about me with great effect..."*

RE-EVALUATING THE HAND OF GOD
(YOU ARE NOT ALONE)

The time has come for those who have been pushed aside, overlooked, and made to feel unimportant to begin to re-evaluate the hand of God in their lives. It is so important for every believer to fully comprehend that being a Christian or being good at anything in life will bring you through a pathway called "rejection." Every great past and present leader in the Bible as well as in the country, community, and home today had to face and overcome some type of rejection. Most people only look at the glory and never look at the rejection and shame great men and women of God have been able to walk through. This is the time to look at it and acknowledge that we will all go through one route after another route of rejection. This is the only way to reach the destiny God has ordained for our lives. The thing that will keep you from being stopped or turning back when faced with rejection is understanding that you are not alone.

I Corinthians 10:13 *"There hath no temptation taken you but such as is common to man: but God is faithful, who will not suffer you to be tempted above that ye are able; but will with the temptation also make a way to escape, that ye may be able to bear it."*

The Message Translation says, *"No test or temptation that comes your way is beyond the course of what others have had to face. All you need to remember is that God will never let you down; he'll never let you be pushed past your limit; he'll always be there to help you come through it."*

The Bible is full of examples of those who were rejected and saw the blessings of God come forth as a result of their rejection. It is time for us to learn deep lessons that we've allowed so many in the body of Christ to overlook concerning suffering **rejection**. These lessons are necessary in order to give you experiences that bring hope and comfort to other brethren. Your adversary, the devil, has tried to cause you to feel isolated from those in your spiritual family who have been through the exact same thing. Don't you dare be deceived by his subtility. God will never leave you nor forsake you and He will also allow the brethren to confirm the mighty hand of God in your life.

Romans 15:4 says, *"For whatsoever things were written aforetime were written for our learning, that we through patience and comfort of the scriptures might have hope."*

God is positioning you to receive what he has promised and it is vitally important for you to demonstrate hope or a happy anticipation of good based on this fact; you are not alone. Others faced the same challenges and made it to the other side okay and so will you. It is through this knowledge that you will triumphant over the enemy. The ignorance that you are alone will be eradicated and you will keep others from perishing in the dark.

Hosea 4:6 *"My people are destroyed for lack of knowledge: because thou has rejected knowledge. I will also reject thee, that thou shalt be no priest to me: seeing thou hast forgotten the law of thy God; I will also forget thy children."*

Isaiah 5:13 *"Therefore my people are gone into captivity, because they have no knowledge: and*

*their honourable men are famished, and their multi-
tude dried up with thirst."*

Proverbs 19:2 *"Also, that the soul be without
knowledge, it is not good; and he that hasted with
his feet sinneth."*

As you allow the words of this book to impart knowledge to you, I believe the joy of the Lord will begin to arise in your spirit on your way to fresh experiences with God. Even though you will be rejected, your enlightenment will cause you to continue to move forward in the purpose of the Father. You will have answers and examples that will help you fight the good fight of faith and you will win!

SHOCKED

Rejection usually comes with an element of surprise. The average person struggles with it because they were shocked about who rejected them. I can truly say that one of the most difficult things to deal with about the rejection aspect is who causes you to experience it. Most people rehearse the rejection over and over because they are so surprised by the people who rejected them. In other words, most of the time you will not see it coming. You will probably be expecting appreciation or acceptance from some of the people who will reject you. In the old comedy show "Gomer Pyle," Gomer was noted for shouting out these words to Sgt. Carter; "Surprise, Surprise, Surprise!" Sgt. Carter was always trying to do something to get Gomer out of the marines or out of his platoon. Many times he would think that the scheme he came up with had succeeded, only to look up and hear Gomer's voice. It was a shock to Sgt. Carter to see how Gomer kept coming right back to his platoon. But think about how surprised Gomer would had been if he knew what Sgt. Carter was truly up to. People you love, people you help, and people you desire to help will reject you. Those who you least expect or those you think should understand your assignment will surprise you with rejection. This is the thing that tries to catch you off guard. You must get over the shock. This is what happened to Moses.

Acts 7:24-27 *"And seeing one of them suffer wrong, he defended him, and avenged him that was oppressed, and smote the Egyptian: For he supposed his brethren would have understood how that God by his hand would deliver them: but they understood not. And the next day he shewed himself unto them as they strove, and would have set them at one again, saying, Sirs, ye are brethren: why*

21

*do ye wrong one to another? But he that did his
neighbor wrong thrust him away, saying, Who made
thee a ruler and a judge over us?*

Moses was expecting his brothers to receive his help and ministry, but instead they rejected him. He was told by God to tell Pharoah to let his people go. Moses was chosen by God to lead his people (the Israelites) out of bondage or Egypt. They rejected him because they didn't understand the call of God on his life. The same is true concerning you and I. Many will think you are being arrogant, proud, or self-righteous, but this rejection will be because they are ignorant of God's mandate on your life.

Shock also occurs because of the time of the rejection. Rejection usually happens at a time of celebration or when you least expect it. Many people have been rejected at the height of their success. On their anniversary, a wife is told by her husband that he no longer wants to be married. A husband is told by his wife that she no longer wants to be married six months after they just closed the deal on their new home. A daughter is told to get out after she finally gets her nerves up to tell her parents she is pregnant out of wedlock. A pastor is told by his members that they are moving on right after he just finished building a new place of worship. The situations are too numerous to mention, but the shock is still real and must be dealt with. There will be times you will see rejection coming and other times, you will not. It will come from people and places you were not expecting. You must get over the shock and advance the kingdom of God!

Proverbs 24:10 *"If thou faint in the day of adversity, thy strength is small."*

The Message Translation says, *"If you fall to pieces in a crisis, there wasn't much to you in the first place."*

You must not allow the shock of rejection to break you down. We have all had to face some kind of crisis or another. The size of our strength can never be measured during the smooth times in life. You must function in total assurance and peace in the midst of the adversity. Others may have quit and given in to the crisis, but you are of another spirit. The spirit of Jesus Christ is able to carry you forward. God delights in you and you are well able to stand.

Those who accused you of being just another religious person, are going to see that your strength is big. You have been empowered with mega strength. Those who are waiting to see you lose heart will have to keep waiting because your strength is being revealed during the times of rejection in your life. You will not fall apart and those who love you will rejoice as they see the strength of God exemplified!

SHOCK THERAPY

God, in the times we are living in will have people who will know how to do shock therapy on themselves and others. They will know how to take the word and walk through times of rejection and turn the valleys of weeping to wellsprings of life. These soldiers are going from strength to strength. They will preach with power and conviction based on the sure word of prophecy (the word of God) and the victory they've experienced.

> Psalms 84:5-7 *"Blessed is the man whose strength is in thee; in whose heart are the ways of them. Who passing through the valley of Baca make it a well; the rain also filleth the pools. They go from strength to strength, every one of them in Zion appeareth before God."*

It is important to note that this valley is a valley of weeping (Baca). It is a place of tears. But it is a place that the early rain fills with blessings according to the Amplified translation of the Bible. It is a place where you and I increase in victorious power. You are walking through this rejection to discover the rain from heaven that will help you minister to others who will run into this same valley. The Message Translation says something very profound,

> (Message Translation) Psalms 84:5-7 *"And how blessed all those in whom you live, whose lives become roads you travel, They wind through lonesome valleys, come upon brooks, discover cool springs and pools brimming with rain! God-traveled, these roads curve up the mountain, and at the last turn—Zion! God in full view!*

Many of us can truly agree with this translation. The rejection made us feel alone, but after we walked through it, our view of God is no longer blurred. We see him high and lifted up above every circumstance in our lives.

The thing you must know about the rejection is that God has prepared you for it. Even though you didn't see it coming, the God that you serve saw it coming and God has already tried and tested you for the rejection before it showed up.

> Acts 7:23 *"And when he was full forty years old, it came into his heart to visit his brethren the children of Israel."*

This verse tells us Moses was forty years old before it came into his spirit to visit his brothers. God never uses a number just to use it. **Forty** in the scriptures symbolizes "trial, temptations and tests."

> Exodus 16:35 says, *"And the children of Israel did eat manna forty years, until they came in the land inhabited; they did eat manna, until they came unto the borders of the land of Canaan."*

The word **manna** means "a whatness or what is it." God is motivating his people to eat something they can't understand in order to sustain them through the wilderness. Many of God's people have eaten of stuff they couldn't understand, but they are now ready to go and partake of every good thing God has ordained for their lives. The good news is what hasn't made sense in times past is about to make a whole lot of sense to you.

> Psalms 12:6 declares, *"The words of the Lord are pure words: as silver tried in a furnace of earth, purified seven times."*

Psalms 18:30 says, *"As for God, his way is perfect: the word of the Lord is tried: he is a buckler to all those that trust in him."*

These verses bring us to an awareness that God tests his words and if we are going to be used as a redemptive word to our generations, we must be tested.

Psalms 66:10-12, *"For thou, O God, hast proved us: thou hast tried us, as silver is tried. Thou broughtest us into the net; thou laidst affliction upon our loins. Thou hast caused men to ride over our heads; we went through fire and through water: but thou broughtest us out into a wealthy place."*

The children of Israel were tried and tested before they received God's best and you will be too. Moses had been tried and tested before he experienced rejection. The testing prepared Moses for the increase God had in store for him. He was ready for the rejection and so are you. The rejection caused him to flee from Egypt into Madian. The word **Egypt** means "to limit or set boundaries." The word **Madian** means "brawling or contention." In other words, this rejection caused Moses to move out from among those who limited God and move into a place of spiritual warfare. Whenever you decide to step out by faith, you will run into conflict or warfare. Brawlings and contentions will start to arise from those who are close to you. This is Satan's plan of attack in order to keep you thinking small or cause you to draw back. Don't you dare give in to this tactic at all. You've got what it takes to press forward, so keep moving on.

Rejection also pushed Moses into the presence of a mature man of God by the name of Jethro. Moses stayed under the tutoring of his father-in-law, Jethro for forty years. Mature men of God have the experience you need to move through rejection periods that happen in your life. They bring you the therapy necessary for you to come out of the rejection as a deliverer or spokes-person for Christ. The word **Jethro** means "excellence." God will connect you with men and women who have an excellent spirit once you've endured the warfare of the adversary. Whenever we are tried, we come forth like pure gold and whenever we listen to mature men and women of God, we come out with the excellence of God.

Job 23:10 *"But he knoweth the way that I take: when he hath tried me, I shall come forth as gold."*

The Amplified says, *"But He knows the way that I take [He has concern for it, appreciates, and pays attention to it]. When He has tried me, I shall come forth as refined gold [pure and luminous]."*

We must know it is indeed the will of our Heavenly Father that we walk in his excellence and continue to move towards it. We must accept it as an ongoing process. Our spirit has been made excellent. Our soul is being made excellent and our bodies will be made excellent.

I Peter 2:9 *"But ye are a chosen generation, a royal priesthood, an holy nation, a peculiar people: that ye should show forth the praises of him who hath called you out of darkness into his marvellous light:"*

The word **praises** used in this verse is the Greek word **arete** which means "manliness, valor, virtue and excellence." God called us out of the world's system to display his virtues and perfections. He brought us to this place of excellence through his Son, Jesus Christ.

II Peter 1:3 *"According as his divine power hath given unto us all things that pertain unto life and godliness, through the knowledge of him that hath called us to glory and virtue:"*

The word **virtue** is the same Greek word "arete." It tells us that God has called us to excellence. Yet, many saints refuse to go through the warfare and hearken to the voice of the Jethros the Lord strategically places in their lives. Jethro had the wisdom or insight Moses needed in order to fulfill his destiny. He mentored Moses and gave him the assignment of watching over his flock, which prepared Moses for leading Israel out of bondage.

We definitely need seasoned men and women of God to stand up and be counted for in these perilous times in which we live. Jethro had to be seasoned enough to give shock therapy or help, but Moses had to be seasoned enough to receive the help that was offered. Let me ask you a question; are you ready to meet your Jethro? He may not speak what you want to hear, but he will definite speak those things that will add virtue to your life.

Proverbs 10:29 *"The way of the Lord is strength to the upright: but destruction shall be to the workers of iniquity."*

The Message Translation reads *"God is solid backing to a well-lived life, but he calls into question a shabby performance."*

We must constantly be reminded that our God doesn't want us to do anything shabby. God does everything well and he expects the same out of his children. We can't expect shabbiness to please our excellent God. Jethro helped prepare Moses with the excellence needed to bring Israel forth. God is bringing the body of Christ into contact with men and women full of excellence to challenge us to a higher dimension in him.

Moses was eighty years old when he saw the bush burning. This means he was doubly ready. **Eight** in the scriptures means "new beginning." I believe this book is being read by some of you who are just like Moses. You've been set up for your new beginning. It is time to go through whatever it takes to see your life receive a brand new start. Your trials and tests have not been in vain. They will bring you to a new beginning that will be ten times better than anything you've seen before.

The number forty is also used in the scriptures as Moses received the law. Again, I remind you that the number **forty** means "tried or tested."

Exodus 34:28 says, *"And he was there with the Lord forty days and forty nights: he did neither eat bread, nor drink water. And he wrote upon the tables the words of the covenant, the ten commandments."*

This is a direct shadow of Jesus who was tempted of the devil in the wilderness for forty days and forty nights while fasting, according to the gospels of Matthew and Luke. I like the way Luke explains it better for the sake of this book.

Luke 4:2,13-14 says, *"Being forty days tempted of the devil. And in those days he did eat nothing: and when they were ended, he afterward hungered. And when the devil had ended all the temptation, he departed from him for a season. And Jesus returned in the power of the Spirit into Galilee: and there went out a fame of him through all the region round about."*

You and I will never walk in the power of the Spirit until we've been tested and rejected. Also, we see God sending Jesus supernatural assistance to minister to him.

Matthew 4:11 declares, *"Then the devil leaveth him, and behold, angels came and ministered to unto him."*

In other words, Jesus had been supernaturally prepared for the rejection he was about to face as he went forth preaching and teaching the gospel of the kingdom. God, as an All-Knowing Master has prepared you for the rejection you've gone through and will go through. For every time people turn deaf ears on the words of life you're trying to give them, you've been made ready. For every relationship you thought would last and it didn't, you've been made ready. For every one you tried to lift up and they rejected your hand, you've been made ready. Maybe you didn't feel ready when the rejection happened, but the truth of the matter is you are more ready than you think. You have been given the Holy Ghost, the word of God, and the assistance of angels to build you up for this moment. You are ready and you can make it through.

I have a saying that I always say to the members of the church, "preparation is never a waste of time." I believe that you've been made ready to bring healing and guidance to others. The days, weeks, months, and years gone by have gotten you ready to be a physician of healing to others. You didn't spend a second of your life in vain. You are going to give massages of hope that will push others into a great future. You will know exactly where to pour the oil and lotion to cause the minds and hearts of others to be relaxed. They will hear your words and get up refreshed for the task at hand. You will offer them words that will stimulate their souls. You are a qualified therapist!

HATED WITHOUT A CAUSE

If you were to ask the average person who rejected someone, whether they hated the individual whom they rejected, they'd probably answer "no." However, let's closely examine the definition of rejection. The word **rejection** means "to spurn, refuse, view as vile, despise, cast away or cast off." It means "to disdain, disappear, disapprove, separate, and disallow." These definitions alone are words of pain and sorrow. They are synonymous with the word "hate." For those who despise you or want to see you disappear, how can they say that isn't hate? These definitions are totally opposite of the way we are told by God to treat men. Yet, we see people who treat men like this all the time. People who hate what the Father is doing in your life will hate you without a cause. I am still amazed at how people who don't know you or you've never mistreated, could just hate you. Still, I recognize that the scriptures must be fulfilled even those scriptures that seem painful.

Psalms 35:19 *"Let not them that are mine enemies wrongfully rejoice over me: neither let them wink with the eye that hate me without a cause."*

Psalms 69:4 *"They that hate me without a cause are more than the hairs of mine head:..."*

Psalms 109:3-5 *"They compassed me about also with words of hatred; and fought against me without a cause. For my love they are my adversaries: but I give myself unto prayer. And they have rewarded me evil for good, and hatred for my love."*

St. John 15:24,25 *"If I had not done among them the works which none other man did, they had not*

*had sin: but now have they both seen and hated
both me and my Father. But this cometh to pass,
that the word might be fulfilled that is written in
their law, They hated me without a cause."*

Every honest and just man knows that Jesus was perfect and upright. Yet, we see people hating him for no reason at all. He was rejected without a cause and was aware that the word of God had to come to pass.

Isaiah 53:3 *"He is despised and rejected of men; a
man of sorrows, and acquainted with grief: and we
hid as it were our faces from him; he was despised,
and we esteemed him not."*

We aren't greater than Jesus, so we can expect the same treatment. Jesus never allowed the strife or contentions of men to destroy his character. We must remember that our God will not make people hate us, but he will use this as an opportunity to demonstrate and develop our character.

Moses was brought out of Egypt (limit) into Madian (strife) which caused him to be one of the meekest men to walk the face of the earth. God will use your "haters" to make you a mild-tempered woman or man of God. I've seen members in the congregation I pastor who haven't done anything but serve and strive to bless people, but the relatives of those people hate the members of my congregation. A few incidents immediately come to mind.

A member in our congregation years ago was having a house warming to celebrate moving into her new apartment. She and her husband had separated under some very distasteful circumstances, but we were excited that God had blessed her and her beautiful daughter with a place to stay. My wife and I arrived to the celebration a little late due to our other pastoral duties. When we did arrive, we saw cars and people everywhere. As we walked up to go towards the apartment, we greeted everyone we saw. Whether we knew them or not, we spoke politely to them as we acknowledged their presence. We saw some of the kids playing kick ball, basketball, throwing Frisbees and enjoying themselves. It seemed to be a happy occasion, until my wife and I approached the crowd sitting down under a shade tree in the yard. We spoke to everybody in the crowd and hugged the necks of those we were familiar with. As we were doing so, I heard this lady begin to gripe and grumble to some of the others sitting near her. She had a look of total resentment toward my wife and I. We knew that hateful look because as leaders, we've seen it many times. My wife informed me that she was the sister of the young lady in our congregation. This caused me to strive to do even more to rid her of the hatred I saw, but nothing was moving this lady.

My wife and I left them sitting under the tree and proceeded to speak to those inside the house, including the host for the afternoon. Everyone was friendly and excited, but my mind was still trying to figure out why this lady under the tree had such a cold and unloving spirit towards my wife and I. As we were walking from the house to speak to those saints we saw on the basketball court, I asked my wife did she say anything to the woman that I didn't know about. She immediately said "no." I asked the saints on the court had they said or done anything to the lady before we arrived so I could be aware of it and understand this woman's behavior. They stated that they hadn't done anything. They said the lady had been acting like that all day long.

Eventually, as the day continued, an incident occurred on the basketball court and this lady went off. She said, "That's what's wrong with those church folk; they want to take over. They think they are so much better than everybody else. They are coming here trying to take over everything. They took over the kitchen; now they are taking over on the court.

I don't know who they think they are." She left the place in a rage, acting unseemly. Her relative said to us, "Pay her no mind. She does this kind of thing all the time. It is not your fault, but it is just the way she is." So, we continued to play and have fun. The rest of the day went smoothly. We played volleyball, ate and enjoyed her other saved and unsaved relatives.

Another incident that comes to mind is concerning a young lady who was a part of our congregation whose mother (for no reason at all) said, she didn't like the people in our church. Yet, the people in the church have helped her daughter time and time again when her daughter was sick. We've helped this same lady pay light bills to stay warm in the winter. Saints sacrificed time and time again to carry her daughter (who was a member of the church) to the hospital, when she needed to go. This sister's mother hated without a cause.

The final incident that I will choose to mention happened in a church service. I was preaching in Raleigh, North Carolina and a particular pastor was present. I noticed as I was introduced that he had an unpleasant spirit towards me. I knew I had never met him or if I had, I didn't recall meeting him. As the word of God began to go forth in power and demonstration, his countenance began to change. At first, I felt hate coming from him towards me, but the word of God and the presence of God caused him to conform to the image of Jesus. The message ended and the service dismissed as many people were delivered through the word. This man of God came up to me and said, "Pastor Sharpe, I don't know you and have never met you, but I had heard of your name and I didn't like you, but now I like you and appreciate God using you for his glory." In other words, he hated me without a cause.

This type of attitude reveals the immaturity of some people. Whether you are a leader or not, you should never hate someone you haven't even met. How can you say you hate certain doctors, lawyers, television preachers, and gospel singers you've never met? Satan is tying to deceive you in order to cheat you out of a divine connection you might need in your life. Step up and walk in the love of God!

Proverbs 17:17 *"A friend loveth at all times, and a brother is born for adversity."*

The Message Translation says, *"Friends love through all kinds of weather, and families stick together in all kinds of trouble."*

You and I must not get caught up in hating people. We must show ourselves friendly. We must love without respect of person. We must see everybody as a valuable commodity. When people disagree with our religious views, we must love them. Or when they choose to serve another God besides the true and living God, we must love them. This doesn't mean we are compromising, it just means we respect their God given right to choose.

God isn't intimidated by their choice and neither should you be. The love of God you demonstrate can turn them away from error. You must show them that you are mature in love. Your love is based on knowing your God created them and wants them to be delivered.

Jeremiah 31:3 *"The Lord hath appeared of old unto me, saying Yea, I have loved thee with an everlasting love: therefore with lovingkindness have I drawn thee."*

REASONS FOR BEING REJECTED

I will now strive to look at reasons for being rejected or cast off. Some of these will bear witness with where you are in your relationship with God and others. It is my hope that as you identify or locate the reason for the rejection that you will stop crying about it and walk in the authority you've been given as a believer in Christ Jesus.

> Luke 9:22 *"Saying, The son of man must suffer many things, and be rejected of the elders, and chief priests and scribes, and be slain, and be raised the third day."*

This verse again shows us that Jesus, the pattern Son, was rejected, but wasn't afraid or cast down by it. He trusted his Father with his life and he knew that it was necessary to endure rejection before he would be raised. The word **must** used in the previous verse means "there is no way around or avoiding the rejection." I believe we need to understand that we can't run or hide from rejection, but we must face it with boldness and courage. You may say, "I will never be rejected again," but you would be lying to yourself. You must be willing and ready to confront and overcome rejection when it arises.

I hope that as you examine reasons for being rejected you will rise above it into a new place in God. I hope you will notice that Jesus didn't see rejection as the end of his assignment or his life. He saw it as part of his journey to his destination. He knew he was destined to sit at his Father's right hand. He knew he could survive the rejection of the elders, chief priests, and scribes.

This is my admonishment to you as a believer in Christ. You have much to offer this untoward generation. They need the deposit that is on the inside of you. Even though they think they are fine without it, you must see beyond their ignorance and the mask they have on and offer them the good news of Jesus Christ. You must see yourself as an answer to the dilemmas of our nation. This is why you must pay close attention to the reasons rejection occurs, so you will have the ability to press on.

#1
YOU ARE A PIONEER

One reason some people experience rejection by others is because they are stepping out into brand new territory. They are attempting to do something that no one in their family or community has done. Whenever you step out by faith and attempt something new or different, you will be rejected. People will reject you then because what you are attempting to do seems crazy or far-fetched. Many saints have heard the Lord speak ideas to their hearts and they are too afraid to carry them forth because they haven't seen anyone in their family attempt such a thing. We must not let fear cripple us in this fashion. We must know that God is willing to use a pioneer to step out and do it. Yes, people will disdain you and disapprove of what God said, but once you've followed proper protocol and received guidance from those who have rule over you, it's time to go for it.

> Mark 2:12 *"And immediately he arose, took up the bed, and went forth before them all; insomuch that they were all amazed, and glorified God, saying, We never saw it on this fashion."*

Jesus was willing to do something that the people had never seen before when he walked this earth. He is still willing to work through us like that today. Too many of us are sitting back waiting for somebody else to do it before we make an attempt to try. God is saying, "you're the pioneer that I have chosen for this hour and the time is now!

Noah is a good example of this. He was warned by God and built an ark to save his house. He called out to others, but they rejected the call. He found grace in the eyes of the Lord. I know he must have looked and sounded real stupid to those that knew him. Pioneers are willing to look insane for a little while in order to rescue others who are in need of a new beginning. The Wright brothers had to be willing to look stupid and be rejected to believe they could fly in an airplane. They paved the way for the types of airplanes and jets we have today. You may be the first one to write a book or sing in your family, so don't be surprised when rejection shows up.

#2
MAN'S PERVERTED HEART AND MIND

Lot's daughters' rejection is an example of the perverted hearts and minds of men. Lot who was a preacher of righteousness was determined to honor and respect the angels who were guests at his home in the land of Sodom and Gomorrah. He was willing to release his daughters to the men of the city instead of the angels. The men rejected his daughters and tried to break the door down, but the angels pulled Lot into the house and smote the men at the door with blindness. When people have perverted hearts and minds, they will reject what is natural for the unnatural. Some men are rejecting their wives in order to join with another man. Some women are rejecting their husbands in order to join to another woman. This type of rejection is being pushed on our society by the media, but the church must refuse to endorse this type of behavior.

I believe that Lot's daughters were beautiful to look upon, but when a man's heart and mind has been warped, he can't see what he needs to see. The Bible plainly tells us that Lot's daughters were virgins.

Genesis 19:8 *"Behold now, I have two daughters which have not known man;..."*

God wants us to adjust our thinking to his. He is not going to adjust his thinking to ours. God honors marriage, but every kind of music and lifestyle that doesn't promote it, is in error. Society is constantly being bombarded by television shows and videos which promote same sex relationships, but God is lovingly calling man back to the truth.

Jeremiah 17:9 *"The heart is deceitful above all things, and desperately wicked: who can know it?"*

The Message Translation says, *"The heart is hope-lessly dark and deceitful, a puzzle that no one can figure out."*

These verses of scripture cause us to see the need of being born again or being a new creation in Christ. We are in need of a new heart or new spirit. The old one is so deceptive that we can't figure it out. It is like trying to put a puzzle together compiled of five thousand pieces with some of the pieces missing.

It is difficult to figure out what truly satisfies a man who is not in the kingdom of God. The heart is in gross darkness and deception to the point that its decisions are off course. This causes man to choose the wrong thing time and time again. It causes him to reject the righteous things for those things that will lead to a perverted lifestyle.

Proverbs 14:12 *"There is a way that seemeth right unto man, but the end thereof are the ways of death. Even in laughter the heart is sorrowful; and the end of that mirth is heaviness."*

The Message Translation says, *"There's a way of life that looks harmless enough; look again—it leads straight to hell. Sure those people appear to be having a good time, but all that laughter will end in heartbreak."*

These verses speak to the core of our being to show us that the fun involved in sin eventually runs out. The thing that once had you laughing will eventually have you crying. Most of us who have lived any period of time have discovered this potent truth. It is the devil's job to make sin look harmless, but sin leads to death. Commercials and television shows have tried to paint another picture. They glamorize evil in order to persuade men to throw away the values that our great, great grandparents and the word of God hold dear. You and I have to be wise enough to choose God's way. Moses chose to suffer with God's people than to enjoy living in sin for a season.

Hebrews 11:25 *"Choosing rather to suffer affliction with the people of God, than to enjoy the pleasures of sin for a season."*

#3
JEALOUSY, ENVY AND HATRED

Genesis 37:3-5,9-11 "Now Israel loved Joseph more than all his children, because he was the son of his old age: and he made him a coat of many colours. And when his brethren saw that their father loved him more than all his brethren, they hated him, and could not speak peaceably unto him. And Joseph dreamed a dream, and he told it his brethren, and they hated him yet the more. And he dreamed yet another dream, and told it his brethren, and said, Behold, I have dreamed a dream more; and behold, the sun and the moon and the eleven stars made obeisance to me. And he told it to his father, and to his brethren: and his father rebuked him, and said unto him, What is this dream that thou hast dreamed? Shall I and thy mother and thy brethren indeed come to bow down ourselves to thee to the earth? And his brethren envied him, but his father observed the saying."

Great things happen because we serve a great God. These great things should cause a celebration toward God, but sometimes they create hate, jealousy and envy. Joseph was rejected because of his dreams and coat of many colors. His brothers hated him and could not speak peaceably to him. He dreamed again and they hated him more. He dreamed again and his brothers envied him. Joseph's rejection wasn't because he was a bad person, but because his brothers wanted what he had.

The Amplified Version of the Bible translates the word **blessed** to mean "happy, fortunate, prosperous, and enviable or to be envied." Many times because of the Father's hand in your life, you will experience rejection. You can't be blessed without jealous people trying to put you in a pit or leave you for dead. They will want you to disappear, but bounce back anyway!

The word **Joseph** means to "add." His Father added to his life because he loved him. God wants to do the same for your life. He expects you to seek first his kingdom and his righteousness, so he can add things to your life that the Gentiles (heathens) are seeking.

Joseph was also the son that Israel had in his old age. This made his daddy love him and make the coat of many colors. The birth of Joseph revived his father in his old age. No doubt it made the old man feel like he still had it going on. Israel felt young again. His heart was refreshed by the birth of Joseph. This speaks of the fact that some people will become jealous of you because you bring joy to your Heavenly Father's heart. You always seem to have a testimony of His love for you. They will be jealous because you came in the kingdom after they did and you seem to be getting all the attention. They were in the church first, yet the pastor has you more involved on the helps ministry than they are. They've been in the church longer than you, but within five or six years of serving the ministry, you have been promoted. They should be rejoicing, but instead jealousy and envy has caused them to become resentful towards you. They reject you and try to make you feel small.

This happened to my brother and I many years ago when we first got saved. There were other brothers and sisters who had been in the church much longer than we had. We were so glad to be saved that whatever God or our pastor wanted us to do, we were willing to do it. We definitely didn't come into the house of God to ruffle any feathers. We were just grateful and wanted to express our appreciation to God.

Colossians 3:23 *"And whatsoever ye do, do it heartily, as to the Lord, and not unto men; Knowing*

*that of the Lord ye shall receive the reward of the
inheritance: for ye serve the Lord Christ."*

We served our pastor and the ministry in any way we could. Whatever our hands found to do we wanted to do it. We swept the floor, cleaned windows, painted, washed the pastor's car and gave. We were totally committed to helping our pastor's vision come to pass.

Ecclesiastes 9:10 says, *"Whatsoever thy hand
findeth to do, do it with thy might; for there is no
work, nor device, nor knowledge, nor wisdom, in
the grave, whither thou goest."*

Later, we began to drive him wherever he needed to go preach. This created negative conversation from some who were a part of the church before we were members. Their words were often cruel and their stares were harsh, but my brother and I stayed focus. We kept loving them.

#4
YOUR COURAGE AND DARINGNESS AT SUCH A YOUNG AGE

I Timothy 4:12 *"Let no man despise thy youth; but
be thou an example of the believers, in word, in
conversation, in charity, in spirit, in faith in purity."*

The Amplified says, *"Let no man despise or think
less of you because of your youth..."*

Paul told Timothy not to allow anyone to despise him or
think less of him because of his youth. I believe sometimes
we make the mistake of acting like serving the Lord is for
the old and settled. When the truth of the matter is that God
wants to be remembered and regarded by young hearts and
minds. He challenges us to remember him in the days of our
youth.

Ecclesiastes 12:1 *"Remember now thy Creator in
the days of thy youth, while the evil days come not,
nor the years draw nigh, when thou shalt say, I have
no pleasure in them;*

David is a good example of a young boy who loved his
Creator. He was told by his Father Jesse to take food to his
brothers in the army and see how they were faring. Once
David arrived, he heard Goliath tormenting the Israelites.
This caused David to ask what would be given to the man
who would kill the Philistine. His oldest brother named Eliab
heard David speak and became angry. He accused David of
having pride and being full of naughtiness of heart. This
wasn't the case at all. David just knew Goliath had to come
down.

47

Ecclesiastes 12:1-5 in the Message Translation says, *"Honor and enjoy your Creator while you're still young. Before the years take their toll and your vigor wanes, Before your vision dims and the world blurs And the winter years keep you close to the fire. In old age, your body no longer serves you so well. Muscles slacken, grip weakens, joints stiffen. The shades are pulled down on the world. You can't come and go at will. Things grind to a halt. The hum of the household fades away. You are wakened now by bird-song. Hikes to the mountains are a thing of the past. Even a stroll down the road has its terrors. Your hair turns apple-blossom white, Adorning a fragile and impotent matchstick body. Yes, you're well on your way to eternal rest, While your friends make plans for your funeral."*

God wants to use your youth for his advantage. He knows how strong you are. He wants to take advantage of your muscles and vigor. These are to be your most productive years for God. You don't have to wait until you can barely see and hear.

Every year our local assembly takes a church trip out of town together. As we spend time at places like Bush Gardens, King's Dominion, Six Flags, etc., I always see the young people getting excited about the huge roller coasters. The older people on the other hand are usually looking for the safer rides at these parks. Personally, I always play it safe with the bumper cars.

Young people like taking risks and living life on the edge. We must channel their daringness toward God. He wants to use their courage to do exploits. David's brother tried to stop him; but the word of God tells us, David turned away from him toward another.

I Samuel 17:30 *"And he turned from him toward another,…"*

I remember when I was twenty years old preaching the gospel of Jesus Christ in different assemblies and forums. It was so exciting for me, but many times as I would arrive at these places, the older adults would look at me with total skepticism. I had to be strong and very courageous in order to survive their stares. My youth didn't prevent me from obeying God. Your lack of fear needs to be used to stir the people of God up. After you destroy the giant standing in your way, others will arise and spoil their own enemies. You must turn away from those who try to hold you back because you're young. You must turn from the critics and turn in the direction of those who can provide faith solutions to the questions in your life.

#5
WRONG BACKGROUND OR NEGATIVE FAMILY

Many of the vessels the Lord is using are not coming from ideal situations of life. Some are coming out of single parent homes. They are coming out of homes of drug dealers and parents who lacked education. These individuals will be groomed by the Master through rough places. Jephthah was such a man. He was a mighty man of valor, but the son of a harlot.

Judges 11:1 *"Now Jephthah the Gileadite was a mighty man of valour, and he was the son of a harlot: and Gilead begat Jephthah."*

This caused his brothers to reject him. They tried to thrust him out of his inheritance, but a war from the children of Ammon came against the Israelites. They needed Jephthah and they are going to need you.

Judges 11:5-7 *"And it was so, that when the children of Ammon made war against Israel, the elders of Gilead went to fetch Jephthah out of the land of Tob: And they said unto Jephthah, Come, and be our captain, that we may fight with the children of Ammon. And Jephthah said unto the elders of Gilead, Did not ye hate me, and expel me out of my father's house? And why are ye come unto me now when ye are in distress?"*

Your background doesn't disqualify you from being used by God. Jephthah fled from his brethren and dwelt in the land of Tob. The word **Tob** means "good." The enemy caused this mighty warrior to run into a place called good.

Romans 8:28 *"And we know that all things work together for good to them that love God, to them who are the called according to his purpose."*

Many of us are saying that it is good that we didn't come from a wealthy family, so we can truly appreciate the blessings God has given us. It's good that some of us came out of the projects and ghettos because we can't steal His glory. It is good because we had to fight through tough times and obstacles that eventually would be what it would take to be captain over the people under attack. We don't have to be ashamed of our family history.

My grandfather and father were weekend drinkers, but today God has used that to cause me to be sensitive towards alcoholics, drug addicts, and drug dealers. I have seen many males and females delivered by the anointing of God. Your background has been wrong for man, but it has been right for God. He makes the crooked places straight and the rough places smooth.

St. Luke 3:5,6 *"Every valley shall be filled, and every mountain and hill shall be brought low; and the crooked shall be made straight, and the rough ways shall be made smooth; And all flesh shall see the salvation of God."*

The Message Translation says, *"Make the road smooth and straight! Every ditch will be filled in, Every bump smoothed out, The detours straightened out, All ruts paved over. Everyone will be there to see The parade of God's salvation."*

The devil will not be able to stop you with detours nor keep you in a rut due to your background. People will see the salvation or deliverance of God as you defeat the enemy because your ruts have been paved. You're not stuck. God knew you would be the answer to the distress of your generation! It would take someone who had defeated some bumps in the road. It would take someone who in spite of the rejection of men; they would see themselves as a captain of God's army. That someone is You!

#6
PEOPLE DON'T LIKE YOUR MESSAGE

We are not to preach or teach to be liked, but rather to cause growth and maturity for the body of Christ. We know we are to grow up into him in all things. This means that sometimes we will be disliked, hated or rejected because of the message we bring. Paul and the disciples of Jesus were despised because of the message they brought forth. It wasn't popular then and it isn't popular now to tell men and women to repent and believe the gospel. As we declare the will of our Father, we will be rejected by carnal minded people. No, we are not trying to be rejected so we can have rejection as a testimony; it will happen because people resist change.

The word of God is designed to change our way of thinking and doing things. It washes and purifies us. The word must be received with meekness as we lay aside filthiness and naughtiness. The word of God challenges us to walk a totally different way as new creatures in Christ. Those who reject the word miss out on the abundance of God available to us through his Son.

Jesus forewarned his disciples concerning the hatred they would encounter as a result of their message and desire to proclaim him.

St. Matthew 10:22,27,28 *"And ye shall be hated of all men for my name's sake: but he that endureth to the end shall be saved. What I tell you in darkness, that speak ye in light: and what ye hear in the ear, that preach ye upon the housetops. And fear not them which kill the body, but are not able to kill the soul: but rather fear him which is able to destroy both soul and body in hell."*

The mistake we make as believers is that we desire to make friends with the world at the expense of giving them a watered down gospel. We must cause them to understand that being a Christian requires us to forsake our allegiance to the world or the ungodly system and pledge our allegiance to Christ. We must break all ties with unfruitful works and walk as the chosen or elect of God.

> James 4:4 *"Ye adulterers and adulteresses, know ye not the friendship of the world is enmity with God? whosoever therefore will be a friend of the world is the enemy of God."*

The apostle James is comparing a Christian's relationship with the world as committing adultery against God. James is causing the twelve tribes who were scattered abroad to be faithful to God.

> The Amplified says, *"You [are like] unfaithful wives [having illicit love affairs with the world and breaking your marriage vow to God]! Do you not know that being the world's friend is being God's enemy? Therefore, whosoever chooses to be a friend of the world takes his stand as an enemy of God."*

According to the word of God, we are married to God. Our connection to him is through our faith in Jesus. This is maintained through denying worldly lusts and other things that try to choke the word out of us.

> The Message Translation says, *"You're cheating on God if all you want is your own way. If you are flirting with the world every chance you get, you'll end up being enemies of God and his way."*

The preaching of the gospel causes us to come into an awareness of God's way. It causes the eyes of our understanding to be enlightened. We start to move in the hope of his calling and the exceeding greatness of his power. We live far above the level of this world and the demonic powers in it.

> Ephesians 2:5,6 *"Even when we were dead in sins, hath quickened us together with Christ, (by grace ye are saved;) And hath raised us up together, and made us sit together in heavenly places in Christ Jesus."*

The word of God demands that we speak in Christ's stead with boldness and with an uncompromising attitude. We are not seeking to please men, but God, who gave us this divine mandate. Some will reject this type of message because they want to continue to live in sin. But we must remember God put the word in our mouths to speak it in order to set the captives free. Yes, some will reject it and despise you for now, but they will love and appreciate you later.

We must remind ourselves that men love darkness rather than light. They refuse to come to the light lest their evil deeds will be reproved. Jesus told his disciples to expect to be beaten and thrown out of the synagogues for the message they were called to deliver. We must never choose to be popular in the sight of men over the message of truth and deliverance. The truth is to be spoken in love. It will cause the fallow ground of men's hearts to be broken up. The word is designed to not only bring financial prosperity, but it will set you free from those things that Satan has been using to keep you bound.

The message of Jesus Christ will also make people angry because those who are making money off your negative habit can no longer do it. The drug dealer can no longer make money off you since you've been delivered from drugs. The gay bars can no longer make money off you if you're no longer gay. Your deliverance empties their pocketbooks which angers those who want take advantage of your negative habits.

Paul and Silas were put in prison because they cast the spirit of divination out of a woman who followed them for many days. When the men saw that this woman could no longer bring in the type of financial gain that they had gotten accustomed to they were furious. They were not even concerned about the woman's deliverance from soothsaying. They were only angry because the hope of their gains were gone.

Acts 16:19 *"And when her masters saw that the hope of their gains was gone, they caught Paul and Silas, and drew them into the market-place unto the rulers"*

Those of us who have been entrusted with the word of God must preach the word with people's deliverance in mind.

#7
IDOLATROUS WAYS

God Almighty was rejected by the house of Israel as they decided that they wanted a king to judge them like the other nations. Following the ways of God instead of the ways of the world will cause you and I to be rejected. We must not pattern our lives after the ungodly nor sit in the seat of the scornful, but we must imitate God. He is the only true and living God we must worship. He is the ruler we need now and forever!

> I Samuel 8:7 *"And the Lord said unto Samuel, Hearken unto the voice of the people in all that they say unto thee: for they have not rejected thee, but they have rejected thee, but they have rejected me, that I should not reign over them."*

God is different and like no other and he expects us to honor him like we know it. He also expects us to be separate and make a difference between holy and unholy. God, who is holy, allowed them to be given a leader who would mistreat them. We will always have regrets when we reject God. He has the ability and power to show up any false god!

> Exodus 18:11 *"Now I know that the Lord is greater than all gods: for in the thing wherein they dealt proudly he was above them."*

Jethro, the father-in-law of Moses, declares to us in this verse that God showed up all of the Egyptian gods. God is still being exalted above every false system set up by man. He alone will be exalted in our lives!

#8
YOUR PAST

The mistakes of our past can cause people around us to reject us. Even the Bible tells us that there is none good, but one and all have sinned and come short of the glory of God. Yet, many people miss out on their deliverance because they want a perfect vessel. They have past sins, but they are looking for somebody to deliver them who has none. The only person like that is Jesus. Everybody else has a sinful past.

Moses was chosen by God to deliver the Israelites but his past as a murderer almost caused them to miss out. They would have drove Moses away on the basis of his past, but God sent him back to Pharaoh. Sometimes it is the earthly tendency to allow our past to abort our future, but God will not let us off the hook that easy. He will still send us back in the midst of those who know about the sins of our past and bring deliverance through us. This shows off his mercy and proves to the world how gracious God truly is. He is God and he has mercy on whoever he chooses. Those who reject us because of our past do not understand that God is rich in mercy. Moreover, since God is the potter and we are the clay, we can't tell him who to use or not to use. We can't tell the one who formed us what to do. He knows exactly what his intent was when he made us. So don't let ignorant, wicked men hold you in your past. You've been purged from your old sins, and it's time to reach for those things which are before you.

True friends want to see you excel and venture out into new and fresh arenas with the Father. They know you have greatness on the inside of you waiting to be awakened. They refuse to rehearse your failures to you. They push you to take the high road by exploring your tomorrow, and not your yesterday. Jethro never mentions Moses' past to him and neither does his daughter who became Moses' wife. They saw the hand of God in his life. The only thing Jethro allowed Moses to rehearse to him was how the Lord destroyed Pharaoh and took care of them in the wilderness. Jethro was then able to rejoice for all the goodness that the Lord had done for Israel.

Exodus 18:10 *"And Jethro said, Blessed be the Lord, who hath delivered you out of the hand of the Egyptians, and out of the hand of Pharaoh, who hath delivered the people from under the hand of the Egyptians."*

You and I can't afford to continue to allow those who are not able to press beyond their past to keep us from pressing beyond ours. God wants to do some exceedingly great things with us, but he can't do them if we stay trapped in the past. Consider the words of Apostle Paul,

Philippians 3:13,14 *"Brethren, I count not myself to have apprehended; but this one thing I do, forgetting those things which are behind, and reaching forth unto those things which are before, I press toward the mark for the prize of the high calling of God in Christ Jesus."*

The Message Translation says, *"By no means do I count myself an expert in all this, but I've got my eye on the goal, where God is beckoning us onward-to Jesus. I'm off and running, and I'm not turning back."*

We should move toward our goals and dreams in spite of the rejection being thrown at us because of our past. The greatness on the inside of you will silence every critic and negative emotion that is trying to abort your destiny if you continue to move forward. Continue to enlarge your tent and lengthen your cords and remember Jesus is not condemning you. He has released you to be a son of God who is accepted in the beloved. Those who are spiritual understand this, but those who are carnal will not. Don't allow their rejection towards you to cause you to miss golden opportunities. God expects you to continue to strain forward to what lies ahead. You haven't possessed it yet, but you will if you continue to reach.

Proverbs 11:23 *"The desire of the righteous is only good..."*

Your desire will lead you straight to the best. You are well on your way. Run towards the finish line with great optimism!

#9
PEOPLE AREN'T BROAD ENOUGH TO DEAL WITH ALL TYPES OF INDIVIDUALS

The beauty about the world we live in is that the people in it come in all sizes, shapes, and colors. I'm glad all aren't one particular color. Diversity is a good thing and causes us to broaden our minds. Jesus died for Jews and Gentiles and he made a way for us all through the shedding of his blood. However, religion and certain denominations don't embrace this. God has a broad scope and isn't willing to let anyone perish. He is reaching out to every man, woman, boy and girl to change them with his love and salvation.

St. John 3:16 *"For God so loved the world, that he gave his only begotten Son, that whosoever believeth in him should not perish, but have everlasting life."*

I John 4:9 *"In this was manifested the love of God toward us, because that God sent his only begotten Son into the world, that we might live through him."*

Some people in the body of Christ hop from church to church because they are not broad enough to love people in the church who see things differently. They can only love a certain type of people. Some who are quiet can only love quiet brothers and sisters. Some who are loud and outspoken can only love those who are loud and outspoken. They fail to understand that the Lord builds the house and places people in the house as it pleases him. It is not up to us who God sets in the house. That decision is God's and God's alone. We must accept the poor, the rich, the wise, the unwise, the strong, the weak, the widow, the single, and the married.

Shallow or narrow believers can't accept whom God sends. The scribes, Pharisees, Sadducees, and the disciples were not always ready to receive the people who were attracted to the ministry of Jesus. Jesus was always ready to receive the religious as well as the prostitute on the street. Peter was taught to receive the Gentiles into the kingdom. He later forgot this lesson and Paul withstood him to his face.

Galatians 2:11 *"But when Peter was come to Antioch, I withstood him to the face, because he was to be blamed."*

We must open our hearts to receive the down and out as well as the up and out. We must be prepared to lift people up no matter where they come from or what race they are. Don't be prejudice. Religious people operate in hate, but we operate in the love of God.

I John 4:11 *"Beloved, If God so loved us, we ought also to love one another."*

We must also broaden our minds as it relates to the opposite sex. Some men can only receive instructions on the job from those of the same sex. We must understand that if your boss is a female and you are a male, you are still under obligation to carry out the orders that are given. God, who is a God of order, has raised up women in the business and political arena who are well qualified for the position. These females shouldn't be rejected because of their sex. They have paid their dues to be in these positions and deserve the same type of respect you would give to the male in the same position.

We must swallow pride and get the qualified in the position instead of those who are incompetent. Male or female should have little to do with the respect we offer an individual once they are legitimately placed in their position as your superior. Since the company has chosen them to supervise that particular department you should co-operate totally.

This is why it is so important for the mind to be renewed by the word of God. Only a renewed mind will enable us to receive who God is positioning for greatness. The mind once it is renewed will not fight God's decisions. It will be broad enough to know and understand that God's choice is the best thing for everyone. Once the mind is renewed all types of individuals will be welcomed and received by you. You will give them your full support in order to see God's best.

#10
YOU DON'T LOOK LIKE MUCH AT YOUR PRESENT STATE

Jesus, the seed of Abraham, who took on the form of a servant was often rejected because he didn't look like much during his earthly ministry. This is what caused people to reject him and believe they were destroying an ordinary man.

I Corinthians 2:8 *"Which none of the princes of this world knew: for had they known it, they would not have crucified the Lord of glory."*

Often we can miss out on a precious thing because we judge things by the natural eye. We fail to discern the person's true worth or value. We reject the true greatness of the Father because we are looking at an unfinished product. Nothing starts out looking as good as it eventually ends up. This is why faith is required. Faith sees what God sees before it manifests itself.

They mistreated Jesus because they didn't recognize who he was. He didn't appear to be anything special, yet he was the long awaited Messiah.

Isaiah 53:1-3 *"Who Hath believed our report? And to whom is the arm of the Lord revealed? For he shall grow up before him as a tender plant, and as a root out of dry ground: he hath no form nor comeliness; and when we shall see him, there is no beauty that we should desire him. He is despised and rejected of men; a man of sorrows, and acquainted with grief: and we hid as it were our faces from him; he was despised, and we esteemed him not."*

I believe you and I are in a world where men and women aren't looking very impressive at the moment, but if you continue to watch, you will see awesome vessels born to change the world. They look small on the outside, but inwardly they are giants in the faith. If you reject them by the way things appear, you will miss out tremendously. Their assignment seems to be small, but it truly is big. The building they are currently in seems to be no larger than your living room, but they are about to explode and break forth on their left and right.

> Job 8:7 *"Though thy beginning was small, yet thy latter end should greatly increase."*

The Lord is not finished with your life and mine. There are those who are taking the back seat now who will be asked to take a front row seat later as the plan of God begins to unfold in their lives. These men and women of God aren't concerned about carrying a title; instead, they would rather carry a towel. They love to serve and help others and God is about to reveal His Masterful plan through them.

> Philippians 1:6 *"Being confident of this very thing, that he which hath begun a good work in you will perform it until the day of Jesus Christ."*

We cheat ourselves out of many divine visitations because we fail to acknowledge the inward greatness in the midst of things that look worthless. The Ark of the Covenant in the Old Testament was carried by the priests and covered with badger skin. This badger's skin covered an ark where God would commune between the cherubims. This is a shadow and type of Jesus Christ. He was God manifested in the flesh. The badger's skin is symbolic of the flesh that caused Jesus to appear to be insignificant and ordinary, but beyond the flesh, Jesus was all God.

There are things that are hiding your true greatness from shining forth, but as you continue to walk with the Lord, those things will be removed. Inside, you are fully aware of God's glory and you must not allow rejection to rob you of your significance. You have a supernatural role to play in the history of the church. Your spiritual and natural life is going to improve and the adversary knows it. Your latter house will be greater than the former. You are passing through the wilderness and fires. Those who see you in a tough place must confirm your destiny to you, not your present state. Those who see you sick must stay excited about your healing rather than give up because of the disease.

On the cross, Jesus looked helpless and powerless, even though he wasn't. When he gave up the ghost and was put in the grave, the disciples thought it was over. They didn't see beyond his present state. He wasn't finished because they put a stone before the tomb and soldiers to watch the grave. He was predestined to get up on the third day. You and I have been ordained to get out of our present situation.

Psalms 34:19 *"Many are the afflictions of the righteous: but the Lord delivered him out of them all."*

Some will look at you in your small or suffering state and begin to count you out. They don't have enough faith to see where you are headed. I thank God today for those men and women who God has used to see beyond where I was in life. Samuel saw a king in David when he was just a shepherd. Elijah saw a prophet in Elisha when he was plowing in the field with twelve yoke of oxen. Jesus saw a mighty apostle in Paul when he was a blasphemer and injurious person.

We must know and understand that God is still molding and shaping the lives of the men and women he has ordained to change the world. Many are in places of ridicule and rejection who will be brought forth into the forefront of what the Father wants to release to their generation. It behooves us to look from the inside out. The woman at the well almost missed a visitation from God, because Jesus looked like an ordinary man. However, she later perceived that he was a prophet and worthy of all the men of the city to come and see. He was the Christ that they had longed for.

Those who are not spiritual will shake their head as you are bearing the cross God has ordained for your life. They can't see beyond what is causing pain to your flesh. They fail to discern that a far more exceeding eternal weight of glory is being brought forth. They are shaking their heads at a single woman who has been rejected by a man. They can't see that God has one who is truly the husband of her destiny. They are shaking their heads at you because you've been rejected by your peers. They can't see that God is going to use you to one day be their pastor. They are shaking their heads at your child who seems to be in trouble in school all the time. They don't perceive that even though your child hasn't been voted most likely to succeed; God has an awesome plan for his life.

This is one of the many reasons God wants to put people around you who understand timing. You may not look like much in the season you're currently in, but you shall come forth like pure gold. Think about Peter, a man who swore and denied the Lord Jesus Christ. Who would have thought he would become one of the greatest apostles to walk this earth, a man whose very shadow would cause people to be healed. All this was locked up on the inside of him and Jesus was able to see it.

Jesus sees beyond the spirit of rejection given to you by carnal minded men. He knows that they are too carnal to recognize your ultimate place of prominence. He wants you to walk through the pain of the cross with great excitement and anticipation. He knows who you truly are even when others don't. He knows the investment he made to set us free from the hand of the enemy. He knows the power of his blood to do a mighty work on our minds and in our spirits.

Hebrews 9:13,14, 21,22 *"For if the blood of bulls and of goats, and the ashes of a heifer sprinkling the unclean, santifieth to the purifying of the flesh: How much more shall the blood of Christ, who through the eternal Spirit offered himself without spot to God, purge your conscience from dead works to serve the living God? Moreover he sprinkled with blood both the tabernacle, and all the vessels of the ministry. And almost all things are by the law purged with blood, and without the shedding of blood is on remission."*

This work is hidden from the natural eye, but it is so powerful that it can spring up when people have counted you out. God waits until they have buried you and pronounced you dead and then allows you to show forth who you really are. This is what really confounds man because they know you according to the flesh, but have no idea of who you are according to the spirit. They think you are a nobody. But hidden beneath all they can see, is a powerful preacher or an anointed worship leader. They think you're a trouble maker, but eventually they will see you speak before kings and governmental officials. Your present state has them fooled!

WHAT ARE THE BLESSINGS
OF BEING REJECTED?

The joy of being a believer in Christ is seeing God turn a negative into a positive. Trust in the foreknowledge of your Father enough to know that he sees a blessing in the rejection you've faced. It is this part of the book that I want you to give close consideration to. I believe God will give you insight or prudence as you read about blessings that will revolutionize your life. It will cause you to function at a higher level of motivation and determination.

Proverbs 14:8 *"The wisdom of the prudent is to understand his way: but the folly of fools is deceit."*

The Amplified says, *"The Wisdom [godly Wisdom, which is comprehensive insight into the ways and purposes of God] of the prudent is to understand his way, but the folly of [self-confident] fools is to deceive."*

The Message Translation says, *"The wisdom of the wise keeps life on track; the foolishness of fools lands them in the ditch."*

As a result of understanding these blessings of rejection, your path will be made plain. You will no longer wonder what is going on because you will see into the ways and purposes of God. Your life will no longer look like it is off track with what your Heavenly Father wants. You can go forth with great determination through what looks like bitter moments.

Proverbs 14:10 *"The heart knoweth his own bitterness: and a stranger doth not intermeddle with his joy."*

The Message Translation says, "The person who shuns the bitter moments of friends will be an outsider at their celebrations."

#1
DRAWS YOU CLOSER TO GOD

James 4:8 *"Draw nigh to God and he will draw nigh to you..."*

The rejection you've faced thus far has caused you to draw closer to your Creator. Rejection causes you not to put your trust in man, but rather in the God who sees and knows all. As people begin to despise and abhor you, you begin to search for your secret place with God. You will find yourself being more aware of his presence and spending more time in fellowship with him. He once again becomes the strength of your life and the joy of your salvation.

The rejection of men drives you into the bosom of your Father and you receive his comfort. The truth of the matter is that most of us grow tremendously during the times of our being disapproved by men. It is at these times that God becomes so precious to us. His love and mercy sustains us and our relationship with him is exalted. Things at this moment are realigned as we see God as our refuge and strength. We once again seek the approval of God instead of the approval of men.

This is one of the reasons why the body of Christ is full of more women than men. Women use their rejection as an opportunity to draw closer to God. They use that divorce as a time to be in the arms of Jesus. They use being made to feel inferior as an opportunity to speak to God and allow God to speak to them. God doesn't just want the woman, but he also wants the man who has been rejected to learn to get the true blessings out of the rejections of life.

David talked about when his mother and father forsook him that the Lord would take him up.

Psalm 27:10 *"When my father and my mother forsake me, then the Lord will take me up."*

It is wonderful to note that David's trust was in the Lord and he knew how to draw nigh to him. We must remind ourselves that God is a spirit; therefore, something spiritual must be done in order to draw nigh to him. You can't do something natural and get closer to God. The rejection pushes you to pray. It pushes you to read your Bible. It causes you to fast and press upon Jesus in a way that attracts him to you. I love the part of the verse that says, *"...and he will draw nigh to you."* God will respond to your pursuit of him. This verse doesn't say he will hide himself, but it says, "he will draw nigh to you."

Moses who was rejected by his brother was forced to flee Egypt and while watching over Jethro's flock saw a bush burning on the mountain of God, but the bush didn't consume. He decided to turn aside to see. It was when he did this that the Lord saw him and called him. God wouldn't have called out to Moses if he didn't first turn aside to see what was going on with the bush.

We need to turn aside from the agenda of our day to see what God is trying to tell us. We must turn away from what we've been doing day in and day out to experience a closer walk with the Father. God wants us to move away from being so entangled with the affairs of this life and draw close to him. He wants our feet to touch holy ground. He's asking us to take our natural shoes off that we've been using to do our natural labor each day and allow our bare feet to feel the heat of his presence.

God wants to reveal who he is to us, so we can go rescue those in bondage. God has been looking at the affliction of his people and the rejection caused you to draw close enough to receive the instructions you need to go and set others free. You will be close enough to God to lead them into a land flowing with milk and honey. Your tears of rejection and sorrow have pushed you into a more meaningful relationship with the Master.

I have a loving daughter who is very close to me. Many times when I travel places, she wants to go with me. I try to encourage her to stay home and spend quality time with her mom. She cries and says, she wants to go with me. If I go to the store, the cleaners, or the post office, she wants to go instead of staying home and drawing closer to her mother. However, as soon as she experiences pain of any kind she immediately cries out for her mom. I am no longer the center of her little world. She wants her mother. My daughter rushes to my wife's bosom to find relief and comfort. She draws nigh to her mother and her mother draws nigh to her. I've seen this happen over and over again. My wife didn't cause the pain or suffering for my daughter; she was just there when the pain showed up. In the same way, God didn't cause your pain, but he is there for you.

Psalms 46:1 *"God is our refuge and strength, a very present help in trouble."*

The rejection of men causes you to become more dependent on God's presence and power. It is when men try to make us feel small that God steps in and shows us how large He really is. It is at this time we are calling on Him for intimacy and not a natural blessing. We call on Him for fellowship and relationship because we need a friend we can trust. We need someone who loves us for who we are and not our talents or gifts. The rejection has caused us to awaken to the reality that we are his inheritance and he is ours. He answers us with the only appropriate answer—Himself. The rejection left us empty with a void that only God can fill. What a wonderful blessing this is! God is our satisfaction and without him, things cannot satisfy us.

Psalms 16:11 *"Thou wilt shew me the path of life:
in thy presence is fulness of joy; at thy right hand
there are pleasures for evermore.*

Many of us quote this verse time and time again, but
let's examine it closely. As we look at the text we will notice
that David is prophesying concerning the delight Jesus had
in his Father's presence even when he faced rejection and
death. Jesus was assured he would be fine. He looked to his
Father. He was satisfied by the Father's presence. Instead of
overeating, shopping, or becoming victimized by rejection,
we should learn from Jesus. We should go to our secret place
with the Father for a greater place of intimacy with Him.

Psalms 73:28 *"But it is good for me to draw near
to God: I have put my trust in the Lord GOD, that I
may declare all thy works."*

The psalmist was declaring the importance of being close
to God. He knew those who are far from God would perish.
He knew it was good to live in close relationship with God.
He didn't say it was good for God. He said it was good for
him. We experience life (peace and joy) at another dimension when we are close to God. However, we will perish
without Him.

God wants to be wanted. Notice, I didn't say that God
needed to be wanted, but rather that He wants to be wanted.
We tend to want God more when the systems around us fail
or when people reject us and we are left alone. It is at these
moments (when God who has been wanting to draw close
to us) is then sought by us with a greater intensity. This is
not the way it should be, but the truth of the matter is most
people function at this level. The children of Israel cried
out to God due to the rejection and hard taskmasters who
afflicted them.

Exodus 3:7 *"And the Lord said, I have surely seen the affliction of my people which are in Egypt, and have heard their cry by reason of their taskmasters; for I know their sorrow."*

The children of Israel drew nigh unto God and God drew nigh unto them. The rejection doesn't have to break you down. It can cause you and God to begin a fresh rendezvous. You can allow your craving for Him to become so intense that it will put lukewarm people to shame. You will look back at the closeness that you and your God have and say, "I thank God for the rejection."

You may be offering people love and they are operating as your adversaries, but your prayer life becomes more and more meaningful to you. Let's look again at the potent words of David.

Psalms 109:4 *"For my love they are my adversaries: but I give myself unto prayer."*

It is prayer that keeps you in your Father's love. This is why God tells us to pray for those who despitefully use you. Without prayer, you and I will get out of the love of God.

Jude verse 20,21 *"But ye, beloved, building up yourselves on your most holy faith, praying in the Holy Ghost, Keep yourselves in the love of God, looking for the mercy of our Lord Jesus Christ unto eternal life."*

The Amplified says, *"But you, beloved, build yourselves up [founded] on your most holy faith [make progress, rise like an edifice higher and higher], praying in the Holy Spirit"*

The apostle Jude talks to us about praying in the Holy Ghost which keeps us in the love of God. Those of us who are filled with the Holy Ghost with the evidence of speaking in an unknown tongue can truly say that rejection causes you to pray more in the Holy Ghost. We speak in tongues more during times of pressure and suffering because the mind is being fought on every side. The inner man prays at this time more than your outer man. This leads you to a closeness and a knowledge of God you haven't known until this point. You get a chance to communicate with Him, Spirit to spirit. He begins to build you up where you've been torn down or made to feel less than who you have been called to be. Your outer man may be perishing but your inward man is being renewed. This is a good thing because we serve God with our spirit or inner man.

Philippians 3:3 *"For we are the circumcision, which worship God in the spirit, and rejoice in Christ Jesus, and have no confidence in the flesh."*

It's your time to have your own personal revival and get to know God up close and personal! This revival will not be because of a meeting with a well known evangelist, bishop, prophet, or teacher. It will be due to an understanding of the Holy Ghost power within you. He will renew you and cause you and I to be robust men and women inwardly.

You can have this renewal everyday of your life. You don't need a special meeting or building for this. The Holy Ghost will help you make progress today!

#2
TURNS YOU INTO A SERIOUS AND RADICAL WORSHIPPER

There is no way to understand the way a person worships the Lord, unless you've gone through rejection yourself. These men and women aren't concerned about how silly they may appear. They sing and dance with great intensity. Their worship is very sincere with no one to impress. It doesn't matter to them whether there is a crowd or few. Titles and large buildings don't impress them, but they just want to worship the God who held their hand while they were small in the eyes of men. I know because I'm one of them. It behooves us to stop and thank the Lord like we truly recognize where he brought us from!

David was a serious and radical worshipper. He praised God seven times a day. It is David who brought the ark of God up with singing and shouting. He was so serious and radical that it embarrassed his wife. She didn't understand what David had been through to get to the place he was currently in. Many will try to silence and tone down the excitement and enthusiasm we exhibit toward our God. Yet at the football, baseball, or basketball game people aren't being asked to tone it down. They are told to yell louder and urge their team onward. How dare we forget the Lord who brought us out of sin, sickness, and poverty.

The rejection you will experience in life will cause you to lay everything at his feet. It will cause you to be broken and not even care about the critics or gainsayers. You will shout unto the Lord with the voice of triumph because you've seen His hand in your life. One of the first things the children of Israel did once they got on the other side of the Red Sea was give God serious and radical worship and praise.

Exodus 15:1 *"Then sang Moses and the children of Israel this song unto the Lord, and spake, saying, I will sing unto the Lord, for he hath triumphed gloriously: the horse and his rider hath he thrown into the sea."*

We must not allow anyone to cause our celebration and gratitude toward God to cease. Moses and the children of Israel started the celebration, but Miriam and the women took it to an even deeper level. Also, I wish to point out to you that Moses who was the leader of Israel started to sing and praise God. This is not the time for leaders to act as if they are beyond praise and worship. We must remember to lead the way. True leaders understand that God raised us up to be a voice for him and to be an example to the saints. We are servants with a mandate over our lives to give God the glory due to his name.

Miriam didn't allow her title of being a prophetess to swell her head. She caught hold of the praises being sung by Moses and the Israelites and worshipped God like a woman who had lost her mind. She wasn't concerned about looking unseemly or being disrespected by the Israelites. She led the way.

Exodus 15:20,21 *"And Miriam the prophetess, the sister of Aaron, took a timbrel in her hand; and all the women went out after her with timbrels and with dances. And Miriam answered them, Sing ye to the Lord, for he hath triumphed gloriously; the horse and his rider hath he thrown into the sea."*

The praise and worship teams or choirs may get the worship and praise service started, but the congregation must take it to another level. We must move from glory to glory in praising the Lord. I dare you to watch the worship of a man or woman who has been rejected. They put their whole self into it. They clap harder and they stump harder. They can hardly be still once the service begins. They have been through the fire and through the flood. They are grateful to God for bringing them out.

I've noticed if the leader is reserved and conservative about praising God, so will the congregation be. We are commanded to praise God and we should do it with all our might. We don't need to behave as if we've arrived, because we definitely haven't. Some leaders even teach about the benefits of praise, yet they don't praise God themselves. We must practice what we preach when it comes to the area of praise and worship. Before rejection shows up praise God, while rejection is going on praise God, and when the rejection is over praise God!

> I Samuel 2:1 *"And Hannah prayed, and said, My heart rejoiceth in the Lord, mine horn is exalted in the Lord: my mouth is enlarged over mine enemies; because I rejoice in thy salvation."*

Hannah was a lady who felt rejected and overlooked. She caused the rejection she was receiving from her adversary, Peninnah, to work for her good by pouring out her soul to God. God responded by blessing her with a son and she rejoiced in the Lord. She became a serious and radical worshipper who wasn't impressed by anybody, but her God.

It is also interesting to note the meaning of the word **Hannah**. Her name means "favored." God's people who are highly favored are being teased and mocked by those who are in the world who seem to be shining. Yet, we must rejoice because the hand of God's deliverance will show up in the midst of our praise. You might not look like you're favored or feel like you're favored, but rejoice because God said you are. The circumstances of life can't change our name. Her name was Hannah even though she had no child. We must know we are favored whether we have anything or not. I should praise God not because of the things, but because of my name—**Favored!**

I was born again at age nineteen as a junior in college. As a new convert in Christ, I was hungry to learn and one of the first things I learned after receiving the Holy Spirit was to give God praise. My sister, Susan, who was already born again demonstrated this to the upmost. She and Ms. Mary Brown, who I call Mother Brown, would literally begin praising God in the car on the way to the sanctuary. By the time we arrived on the grounds of the church these two would get out of the car and start dancing. Once they walked into the sanctuary, they would break out with more dancing. They were literally acting out the Bible.

Psalms 100:4,5 *"Enter into his gates with thanks-giving, and into his courts with praise: be thankful unto him, and bless his name. For the Lord is good; his mercy is everlasting; and his truth endureth to all generations."*

As a new convert, I imitated their ways. I thought about how I was lost and God's right hand pulled me out of sin. I gave God the praise in the car, on the church grounds, and as soon as I entered the sanctuary. This wasn't a distraction to anyone because we would usually arrive to the sanctuary before the rest of the saints. Mother Brown who drove us to the house of God was very prompt and punctual. We were radical worshippers then and we are still radical today. Mother Brown, who is a woman of God in the local assembly I pastor, is still dancing in the house of God. My sister, Susan, pastors a church in Rocky Mount. She is still praising God.

I still listen at gospel music on my way to the house of God and by the time I get there, I'm in high gear. This is the way the world does. Before I became a believer in Christ, I would smoke marijuana and drink along with my friends before we went to the party or club. We would be high before we got to the place and would indulge in more once we arrived. This was a way to try to ensure ourselves of a good time.

I truly believe that we should be ready before we arrive at the sanctuary. I believe we should come with a spiritual high we've gotten at home and in the car that is added to once we join with the rest of the saints. There's no time to be slothful.

Hebrews 6:12 " *That ye be not slothful, but followers of them who through faith and patience inherit the promises.* "

The Amplified says, "*In order that you may not grow disinterested and become [spiritual] slug-gards, but imitators, behaving as do those who through faith (by leaning of the entire personality on God in Christ in absolute trust and confidence in His power, wisdom, and goodness) and by practice of patient endurance and waiting are [now] inher-iting the promises.* "

We know that God expects us to walk by faith and patience to receive what he has ordained for our lives. But for the sake of this book let's look at the word **slothful**. Slothful comes from the Greek word **nothros** which means "dull, monotonous, unexciting, or something that is slow or sluggish." It means "something that has lost its speed or momentum."

The Message Translation says, *"Don't drag
your feet. Be like those who stay the course with
committed faith and then get everything promised to
them."*

God has been too good and you've been through too
much to act unexcited. You've been through too much to
be dull and sluggish. The devil is a liar! Your worship has a
fire in it because of all the persecution and rejection you've
encountered. Notice the potent words spoken to us by the
Apostle Paul,

Romans 12:11 *"Not slothful in business; fervent in
spirit; serving the Lord."*

God is using this mighty man of God named Paul to challenge the saints at Rome to stay full of life. He is reminding
them not to allow their relationship with God (in the work or
worship of God) to grow stale.

The Amplified says, *"Never lag in zeal and in
earnest endeavor; be aglow and burning with the
Spirit, serving the Lord."*

These words along with the things you've encountered create a fire in your worship that will not go out. Your
worship is not monotonous. You're not just going through
the motions. Your worship is alive and vibrant because of
all those who thought you wouldn't make it and treated you
with disdain. You take nothing for granted. In everything,
you have an attitude of thanksgiving and worship. Refuse to
be hesitant about giving God the glory. Desire to give Him
the praise that He is so worthy of.

Worship God with zeal and passion. Take up the timbrel
and dance!

Exodus 15:20 *"And Miriam the prophetess, the sister of Aaron, took the timbrel in her hand, and all the women went out after her with timbrels and dancing."*

#3
CAUSES YOU TO RELEASE LOVE AND GRACE ON OTHERS

Rejection really jerks the pride out of your life. Those who are God-made men and women are anxious to release love and grace on others. Rejection humbles you and gives God a chance to use you and your testimony in a greater way. Again, I remind you that so many people aren't aware of the rejection they must encounter in order to be usable in the kingdom. They don't have the slightest clue about how to identify with Christ in this way. I believe without rejection arrogance will rule the pulpit rather than God's love and grace. Our nation has experienced hurricanes, floods, and storms that should cause us to be willing and ready to share with one another. We definitely aren't looking for high-minded believers at this moment in church history. We need to hear from those who will not try to keep us ignorant of their pain or sorrow.

Jesus was a man of sorrows. This mean he experienced more than one time or moment of sorrow. Rejection does bring with it a feeling of sorrow and grief, but it causes you to be able to identify more readily with the struggles and pain of others. I am so grateful that God the Father didn't keep us ignorant of it. Instead, God showed us the sufferings of Christ, so we could better appreciate the blessing of his consolation.

II Corinthians 1:3-7 *"Blessed be God, even the Father of our Lord Jesus Christ, the Father of mercies, and the God of all comfort; Who comforted us in all our tribulation, that we may be able to comfort them which are in any trouble, by the comfort wherewith we ourselves are comforted of God. For as the sufferings of Christ abound in us,*

*so our consolation also abounded by Christ. And
whether we be afflicted, it is for your consolation
and salvation, which is effectual in the enduring
of the same sufferings which we also suffer: or
whether we be comforted, it is for your consolation
and salvation. And our hope of you is steadfast,
knowing, that as ye are partakers of the sufferings,
so shall ye be also of the consolation."*

God not only sees what we are facing, but He is aware
of who we must comfort. He comforts us so we not only
have the written word to comfort people with, but an experience that causes us to console others. Because of what we've
gone through, we minister out of a heart of compassion and
understanding that it takes to pull people up. Our words
are not hard, shallow or uncaring, but instead they are full
of sympathy and grace. The words we speak build people
rather than tear them down. As we pull out our testimonies,
they can plainly see that we've been down the path they are
currently walking through. We've been despised and cast
off, but God turned it all into a blessing. We must not allow
others to be ignorant of our suffering.

II Corinthians 1:8 *"For we would not, brethren,
have you ignorant of our trouble which came to us
in Asia, that we were pressed out of measure, above
strength, insomuch that we despaired even of our
life."*

Paul wanted this church to be aware of what he had faced
time and time again. The suffering didn't stop him, it only
proved and validated the sure deliverance of God. So many
who never talk about what God brought them through are
cheating us out of consolations. This is why we shouldn't
desire to be anyone but who the Lord made us, because we

all have some suffering to go through. It is nothing to be ashamed of and must be shared to bring assurance and confidence to others.

> II Timothy 1:8 *"Be not thou therefore ashamed of the testimony of our Lord, nor of me his prisoner: but be thou partaker of the afflictions of the gospel according to the power of God."*

Rejection can be so embarrassing that people are ashamed to say they are affiliated with you in any way. Paul admonishes Timothy not to be ashamed of the testimony of Jesus nor of him. Paul knew comfort and consolation was coming.

Many of us need to understand the release of love and grace that will come out of vessels who are being embarrassed by some of the things they are currently experiencing. They may have gone through places where nobody wants to jump in and join them. Nevertheless, those of us who will say, "we stand with you in this suffering," will receive from the grace on their lives. When they come out, they will have a grace on them second to none.

September 16, 1999 is a date which will always stand out in my life. It was the year hurricane Floyd paid certain cities in Eastern North Carolina a visit to be remembered. I can recall so vividly that night retiring for bed as the winds were blowing the trees, but nothing would get us ready for what we were about to see the next morning. My wife kept waking me up during the night as she looked out the door viewing the winds. She kept asking me what I thought about how hard the winds were blowing. I told her it was going to be alright because the grounds were dry and the trees weren't being toppled. She stayed up, I went to bed, and in the morning she woke me up and told me to look out the window at all the water in our back yard. I was still a little dazed and not fully alert and stated to her not to panic, because she had seen water before. She said, "not like this, you need to look out the window." As soon as I looked out the window I started to speak in tongues. Our bedroom window faced our backyard and it was covered with water. I had never in all my days seen so much water. The water was still rising and about to come up to the window. I rushed to the front door and the water was moving up under the car port where our two cars were. Both automobiles, living room furniture, bedroom furniture and much more were lost due to this flood. It was unbelievable to say the least. There I was feeling as helpless as I had ever felt before in my life. I immediately ran back to the backyard window and I saw my neighbor in boots pushing his boat in the water. I yelled to him in a loud voice to make sure he didn't leave without my wife, daughter and I on his boat. He immediately stated that he wouldn't go anywhere without us. I put on my clothes as fast as I could and told my wife to begin packing as much stuff as she could. I knew we had to get out and try to salvage those things which were very important. We immediately woke our daughter and told her to pack her important stuff as fast as she could. As I rushed back to the front door, my wife followed behind me; I was shocked to see how quickly the water had risen. It was now almost up to the door of the car. My wife wanted me step in the water and get the important car information out of the dashboard of each car. As I was about to step down into the water, I noticed the water was very cold and contained filthy things. She pushed me into the water as it continued to rise every minute of the day. I grabbed everything in the car that I felt was important. I checked the dashboards, seats, and trunks of the two vehicles. The water continued to rise and by the time I entered back into the house with all the important papers, the water had started to enter the cars.

My wife and I continued to pack and place things as high on shelves as we possibly could put them. Once I had done almost everything I could do to save our things, I decided to go outside and help as many as I could. My neighbor and other men were on their way to get us out of our house. I told them we were alright for now, but we needed to get our older neighbors out. We then proceeded to go and rescue them out of their homes. Due to the fact my neighbor had the boat and a high deck on his house, we took everyone over to his place. We had decided that it was impossible to drive any truck or car through water that high. The only escape was through the back woods of the neighborhood. This would mean walking through a muddy, snake infested area but it was our only chance at the moment as the water continued to rise. We didn't know how much it would rise nor when it would level off. We told others who were willing to go with us to come. Some people decided to stay. They stated that they wanted to look out for their things. I tried to tell them we can get some more things, but we can't get another you.

I yelled to my wife from my neighbor's house that we were coming back to get her and my daughter. The men and I walked alongside the boat in order to keep it from turning over. The water was waist high as we walked back to my house and picked up my daughter. We also had a little poodle dog that we took with us on the boat. My wife decided to wait on the next boatload and continued to pack a few more necessary things as we placed others in the boat. Eventually, we returned to get her and we walked through the mud and slime of the woods, up the hill onto 64 highway. Morning Star, a church located in Rocky Mount pastored by R. T. McCarter, sent vans from their ministry to take people wherever they wanted or needed to go. I truly thank God for them. We were picked up by one of their vans and taken to a place of safety.

The next few weeks would be used to speak encouragement to so many people saved and unsaved who had lost everything in the natural they had worked hard to gain. I would encourage them with a word the Lord had dropped in my spirit as I was examining the events of the day. As I was riding in the van, the Lord spoke to my spirit to tell the people that he didn't caused this to happen, but he would give us double for all our trouble. It was alive in my spirit and I spoke it boldly and in faith. My expectations were high and I looked for God to bring every bit of it to past. Needless to say, God did that for me and many others who suffered loss and mixed their faith with the word of God. He didn't just do it for Job in the Bible. God came through for us who are under a better covenant which is established upon better promises.

God took this situation and gave us a chance to minister to thousands of people through television and radio. The opportunity probably wouldn't have been given otherwise, but God used it for his glory. As we returned back to our home days later, the smell was unbearable. Furniture was ruined and many things were shifted around. Some things had been stolen, but we had a word from the Lord and he brought that word to pass. I know what it means to be grateful for tissue, water, lights, soap, and a can of soup. I know how to abound and I know how to be abased. I've learned that whatever state I find myself in, to be content. I have learned that I am sufficient in Christ's sufficiency.

Philippians 4:11-13 *"Not that I speak in respect of want: for I have learned, in whatsoever state I am, therewith to be content. I know both how to be abased, and I know how to be abound: every where and in all things I am instructed both to be full and to be hungry, both to abound and to suffer need. I can do all things through Christ which strengthened me."*

Paul said he was instructed to live in much or in little. We also must know that our lives are more than food and raiment. We must not lay up for ourselves treasure upon earth where moth and dust corrupts. We have to find our true contentment in the Lord Himself. He is the health of our countenance.

The Amplified says, *"I have strength for all things in Christ Who empowers me [I am ready for anything and equal to anything through Him Who infuses inner strength into me; I am self-sufficient in Christ's sufficiency]"*

Pastors who have experienced rejection are able to minister to other pastors in a greater way. Kids rejected by their parents can minister a release of love and grace that will cause healing for those abused and molested. You can't truly build people up if you've never been torn down. The rejection is not working against you, but for you.

Roman 8:28 *"And we know that all things work together for good to them that love God, to them who are the called according to his purpose."*

The rejection is a set-up to heal and bring wholeness to others. People need what you have even though you may not like the route you had to travel to get it. Some of us want to walk in the glory of God by traveling a smooth, easy route, but we must remember God leads us many different ways to get to the destiny He has for our lives. He takes some through the fire, some through the flood, but we must all come through the blood. Don't despise the route he's taking you, but reach out to those who are waiting to hear from you. They will need to hear about the pain you felt and how God's right arm gave you deliverance. Tell your testimony with all assurance that the same God who brought you out will bring them out!

Your fruitful words will cause God's people to get back up and try again.

The same grace of God which didn't allow you to stay down too long, will assist them and put them back on their feet.

> Proverbs 24:15,16 *"Lay not wait, O wicked man, against the dwelling of the righteous; spoil not his resting place: For a just man falleth seven times, and riseth up again: but the wicked shall fall into mischief."*

> The Message Translation says, *"Don't interfere with good people lives; don't try to get the best of them. No matter how many times you trip them up, God loyal people don't stay down long; Soon they're up on their feet, while the wicked end up flat on their faces."*

#4
GIVES BIRTH TO NEW THINGS

Another tremendous blessing of rejection is that it causes us to give birth to something new. Many times the rejections of life cause us to help people we didn't know or go places we've never been to apprehend things we've never apprehended before. Moses experienced rejection that caused him to go down into Madian where he met his lovely wife who gave birth to two sons. The Bible plainly teaches us that by the mouth of two or three witnesses shall every word be established. The rejection will cause you to give birth to the new things God has established for you before the foundation of the world.

We need also to note the names of Moses' sons. One was named Gershom and the other was named Eliezer. Moses named the first son **Gershom** which means "expulsion or stranger there." He named the second son **Eliezer** which means "my God is my help." These two sons names reveal to us a process of God that is potent. God will allow you to be rejected or expelled by people, but he will show you that he is your helper. This means we don't have to be covetous. We can move forward knowing God will do something brand new in our lives as a result of rejection.

Paul experienced trouble, fights, and fears, but the God he served came through with great consolation. This is one of the reasons I believed his preaching reached and still reaches so many people today. He didn't hide from us the persecutions and pains he experienced, but exposed us to the comfort that God can bring.

II Corinthians 7:5,6 *"For when we were come into Macedonia, our flesh had no rest, but we were troubled on every side; without were fightings, within were fears. Nevertheless God, that comforteth those*

> *that are cast down, comforted us by the coming of Titus"*

The Message Translation says, *"When we arrived in Macedonia province, we couldn't settle down. The fights in the church and the fears in our hearts kept us on pins and needles. We couldn't relax because we didn't know how it would turn out. Then the God who lifts up the downcast lifted our heads and hearts with the arrival of Titus."*

The casting down you've experienced will cause you to be bold enough to step out into new territory. It is through the rejection that you start being more concerned about what God thinks of you instead of what carnal minded men think of you. Rejection causes you to approach life with an, "I have nothing to lose and everything to gain attitude." You make a decision to move away from the old into the new arenas of life God has prepared for you. Your eyes, mind and ears become keenly aware of fresh relationships and places God wants to bring you into. The great things you once walked by, you now notice. You are now open to the fact that God has ordered your steps and he is indeed your help. God proves to you that He is bigger than the fears you feel inside and will remove the wrong people and send the right people into your life. God sent Titus to comfort Paul and He will send strong anointed believers to comfort you. The word **Titus** means "protected." He was protected by God and was sent to help protect the assignment on the life of Paul by being a comfort to him. God will always protect the investment He knows is on the inside of you. He values you and the ability He has given you. He will not let you die without releasing it to bless others. God is bringing those alongside you who can reaffirm who you are and help protect the anointing.

In spite of all the rejection and pain, the apostle Paul saw new, great, and effectual doors open. The adversaries were many, but the new things kept him excited and on the cutting edge of God. He was always looking for new opportunities to bring people into the kingdom of God. Those who are being rejected are being set up for new opportunities of spreading the gospel of Jesus Christ. We have the sensitivity and grace to walk through doors that we didn't have open before. You have been qualified by the way you've been treated. Their disapproval of you has brought God's approval on you. You are now qualified to do something that hasn't been done before. God has you in this third trimester of life and you will push forth that which will remove your shame and disdain. You can no longer be trapped by the old patterns and mindsets that have caused so many believers to duplicate failure. The old will have no glory because of the greater glory of the new things being birth!

Haggai 2:9 *"The glory of this latter house shall be greater than of the former, saith the Lord of hosts: and in this place will I give peace, saith the Lord of hosts."*

The Amplified says, *"The latter glory of this house [with its successor, to which Jesus came] shall be greater than the former, says the Lord of hosts; and in this place will I give peace and prosperity, says the Lord of hosts."*

The Message Translation says, *"This Temple is going to end up far better than it started out, a glorious beginning but an even more glorious finish: a place in which I will hand out wholeness and holiness."*

This is the type of faith God desires to see in his chosen vessels. This is the only way to achieve in the midst of being rejected. You got to believe a more glorious thing is being wrought. You've got believe the rejection will bring you to a place of wholeness and holiness. It will cause you to separate yourself from the corruption in our world in a way you've never been separated before.

This type of separation is not forced upon you, but is stirred and ignited by the exciting expectation of the glory that awaits you. Joshua challenged the children of Israel to get up and sanctify themselves because of the new things God was about to do.

Joshua 3:5 *"And Joshua said unto the people, Sanctify yourselves: for to morrow the Lord will do wonders among you."*

You must see that what you are going through now is nothing in comparison to the glory which God will reveal in your life. There is something astronomical on the horizon for you!

II Corinthians 4:17 *"For our light affliction, which is but for a moment worketh for us a far more exceeding and eternal weight of glory."*

#5
RELEASES REVELATION

The unfolding of the mysteries of God is the fifth blessing of rejection I wish to discuss in this book. Revelation is born out of hunger and need. God unfolds his word in a greater way at this time in your life because of your desire to know. Rejection and ignorance must not walk together in your life. The rejections of life causes you to ask questions. It is in your search for answers that revelation is born. Revelation is the unfolding of the mysteries or secrets of God. It is when the Holy Spirit makes known unto us the things that eyes have not seen and ears have not heard.

I Corinthians 2:9,10 *"But as it is written, Eye hath not seen, nor ear heard, neither have entered into the heart of man, the things which God hath prepared for them that love him. But God hath revealed them unto us by his: for the Spirit searcheth all things, yea, the deep things of God."*

Paul knew that many people didn't recognize Jesus as the Son of God. He knew that flesh and blood couldn't reveal this mystery, but only the Holy Spirit. He knew the natural-minded man couldn't receive these mysteries, for they are foolishness to him. Paul knew these hidden truths are spiritually discerned.

Paul preached the gospel that he neither received of man nor was taught by man. He got it by revelation. It pleased God to reveal or make known His Son in him. He walked in the glory of revelation. God expects his children to live in those things that he reveals to us.

Deuteronomy 29:29 *"The secret things belong unto the Lord our God: but those things which are revealed belong unto us, and to our children for ever, that we may do all the words of this law."*

The Message Translation says, *"God, our God, will take care of the hidden things but the revealed things are our business. It's up to us and our children to attend to all the terms in this Revelation."*

Believers who experience difficulties discover things in the word that others seemingly miss. They are never blown away by the praises of men because they've seen how quickly those praises can change into insults and persecutions. Instead, these believers are in awe of the mysteries of God. They become good stewards of the mysteries and are faithful to share them with those who are anxious to hear them. These believers have gone through things that forced them to look to God for answers. Out of their extreme pain and rejection have come secrets which have revolutionized their home, church, community, and nation.

Words to great songs, books and sermons are born out of rejection. The rejection forced you into a place of isolation and gave you an opportunity to hear God speak these secrets to you. You begin to understand what you are going through and why you had to go through it as revelation from the Father begins to flow. These hidden truths provide you with the grace you need to thrive in the midst of the disapproval of men.

I remember as a child growing up in the projects, my family and I lived in apartment 81 Eastside Homes in Tarboro, North Carolina. I had a loving mother and father who did a tremendous job with my sister, my brother, and I. My father was a great provider and loved us dearly. He had only one major flaw that eventually ruined his life. He would get drunk every weekend and behaved very violently toward my mother. It usually started on Friday evening once he got paid and continued through Sunday evening. He would sober up in time to go to work Monday and remain sober until Friday evening. My brother and I would often become the brunt of people's jokes. You can't even begin to imagine the hurt and sorrow young boys go through because of your father's negative habit. I remember constantly being teased in the stores and on the playground. It was devastating. Yet, knowing I had the love of my mother, my sister, and my brother, I persevered. I recall the times when our mom would tell my brother and I to go out and see if we could find our daddy, because he would sometimes get drunk and fall. Sometimes we would find him lying on the ground after he had been jumped by somebody in the neighborhood. We would pick him up and dust him off. Sometimes we would have to wipe blood off his brow. My brother would get on one side of him and I would help hold him up on the other side. He would place his arms around our necks and we would help him make it home. This would prove to be prophetic revelation because today my brother and I are pastors and we've had to nourish and encourage many who were hooked on drugs and alcohol.

My father's continuous cycle eventually lead to my parent's separation. My mother finally couldn't take the physical and verbal abuse anymore. While they were separated my dad would always visit us or we would see him in town. Our mother told us to always love him and show him respect because in spite of his drinking habit he was still our father. We didn't have any problem at all with that because our love for him was so great. Later in life my sister and I attended Shaw University, in Raleigh North Carolina. She became a Christian as a freshman in college. I went to college as a sinner and remained unsaved until my junior year. This was a turning point in my life because I received a phone call from home concerning the death of my father. I remember how unbelievable it sounded to my ears. I remember standing by the phone in the hallway at the men's dorm knowing that God didn't kill my father. It had to be the devil who was to blame. My father had given place to Satan and the adversary took his life. He was found dead in a house that had been burned to the ground. The only identifiable remains were his teeth.

I asked the Lord the question, "Lord, how do I get back at this devil for killing my daddy." God responded with a revelation that has forever stuck with me even until this day. He said, "Give me your life and preach my word. Every time you help men and women get delivered off drugs and alcohol you will be getting back at the devil." Well needless to say, I have been getting back at the devil every since. It has been so exciting to see people delivered from drinking, crack, heroin and other drugs.

My brother who also attended Shaw is also seeing God break yokes through him. He has also seen men and women delivered mightily from these strongholds. We both have a revelation of love and compassion in this area; I believe primarily because of our father.

During the times of rejection, God floods your spirit with light. He enlightens you with an abundance of revelation that will amaze or cause men to marvel. You speak heart-felt words that will cause the mouth of the hearers to water. They will want to hear more and more because you are not speaking from your natural head, but you are speaking from your inner man. God is making things known unto you that He reserved for the tough times in your life. I'm so glad God doesn't tell us everything in one encounter with Him. Instead, He waits for the appropriate times in our lives and reveals things as we are able to receive them or in need of them. As we continue to walk with God, He gives us a chance to know something about His name and nature that we never knew before.

Another important thing to know about revelation is that it always takes you up. It does for you the total opposite of rejection. Rejection pulls you down, but revelation encourages and motivates you. Rejection causes the mind to experience a downward spiral. Without revelation being given to you by the Father, your mind would be swamped with so many negative things that you wouldn't survive. But thank God for revelations that lift our head above every circumstance and propels us forward. Revelation empowers our minds and causes us to be able to think good thoughts. Through revelation, we think thoughts of peace and prosperity. The enemy will try to bring the incidents back to your mind that cause you to feel rejected, but God through the power of the Holy Spirit will reveal words that lead to life. These words go deep within you and raise your faith. You must remember God will always talk to you about your next level or next dimension at a time of a crisis. Before the rejection you had everything figured out, but now you have to depend on revelation. You can't go by sight at all. You can only go by revelation. This will not feel like a good place at first, but as you continue to walk with God when pain and rejection show up, you will never look to man first; you will look for revelation. Even if you've been rejected lately, look for revelation. If you've been rejected by your spouse, look for revelation. If you've been rejected by people on your job, look for revelation. God will reveal to you more things about Jesus Christ and your assignment as you walk through the fires of rejection.

Proverbs 3:32 *"For the froward is abomination to the Lord: but his secret is with the righteous."*

Proverbs 3:32 (Amplified) *"For the perverse are an abomination [extremely disgusting and detestable] to the Lord; but His confidential communion*

*and secret counsel are with the [uncompromis-
ingly] righteous (those who are upright and in right
standing with Him)."*

We, who are born again, can walk in a dimension of
revelation unknown to man. His counsel will cause us to
endure and win in life!

#6
MOVES YOU FROM WHAT DOESN'T BELONG TO YOU INTO THE GOD ORDAINED STUFF

Many of us are so hasty to grab and cleave to things God never intended to be a part of our lives from the onset. His plans for us are so huge that unless we truly trust him, we will shortchange ourselves. He knows our down sitting and our uprising. It is knowing this truth which will lead you to a peace second to none. So many of us are missing out on what God ordained and getting what we want. However, what God has ordained is the only thing that will bring true joy and fulfillment. I have learned that the only thing I want for my life is what the Father has ordained.

Certain people and things will not move from you. You will have to ask them to move or be moved from the situation. A good example of this can be seen in the Apostle Paul's life. Paul started out preaching to the Jews, but God ordained that he would preach the gospel to the Gentiles. Once the Jews continued to reject his message, he turned to the Gentiles (which was where God wanted him anyway). The rejection moved him from what didn't belong to him and positioned him to reach those who God ordained for him to reach.

Acts 13:45-48 *"But when the Jews saw multitudes, they were filled with envy, and spake against those things which were spoken by Paul, contradicting and blaspheming, Then Paul and Barnabas waxed bold, and said, It was necessary that the word of God should first have been spoken to you: but seeing ye put it from you, and judge yourselves unworthy of everlasting life, lo, we turn to the Gentiles. For so hath the Lord commanded us, saying, I have set thee to be a light of the Gentiles, that thou shouldest be for salvation unto the ends of earth. And when the Gentiles heard this, they were glad, and glorified the word of the Lord: and as many as were ordained to eternal life believed."*

We must be willing to allow the rejections of life to bring us to what the Father wants us to truly have. Paul went from preaching to those who didn't want to hear the message to those who were glad to hear it. Too many believers are crying and wasting time being rejected by someone God never intended for them to be rejected by. It is especially true for women because women desire to support and nurture. They have been ordained by God to help. The only problem is that you can't help a man who doesn't see you as a good thing. If Paul had not turned away from the Jews he would have been allowing the Jews to abuse him and his assignment.

We shouldn't allow the rejection to continue until it becomes abuse. Instead, we should move into the God ordained place with the God ordained people. In the early years of the ministry, we were conducting services on Granville Street in Tarboro. It was a very small storefront building. The rent was only seventy-five dollars every month. We saw the hand of God in the facility, but eventually the landlord wanted more money. He received a higher offer from another tenant and didn't quite know how to explain it to me. I knew we had been faithful with the place. We had put a lot of hard work in fixing the place up and causing it to look nice as a place of worship. So when we were told we had to leave, I knew it wasn't fair or just; however, I left with a positive attitude. I didn't know all God was doing, but I wasn't afraid to trust him.

Nahum 1:7 *"The Lord is good, a strong hold in the day of trouble; and he knoweth them that trust in him."*

We moved from Granville street to Dowd street in Tarboro. The facility on Dowd Street was bigger and better. It pushed my faith to another level. The rent at that time was two hundred and fifty dollars every month. As time went by, the city of Tarboro had need of the facility. They purchased it from the landowner and told us we would eventually have to start looking for another place of worship. Mr. Chapman who was in charge of asking us to move was very nice about it. I will never forget how he told us that he would never put a man of God out of a building. He stated that he totally believed if he cursed us, God would curse him.

This gave me an experience to work with. I told my wife that this was God's way of bringing us into our own. I told her it was now time for us to buy some land so no one could ask us to move again. As we started to look at the price of property in the city, God opened up a door for us to buy 1.4 acres of land on Albemarle Avenue. Since then we've also acquired 11 acres on Main Street with much more to come. The point I'm trying to get across to you is the rejection pushed us into what God has ordained for the ministry.

Many ministries start out with some of these same experiences. Sometimes we are so comfortable with the small amount of rent we have to pay that we fail to reach out for the God ordained property. God doesn't want us to rent buildings and apartments all our lives. He wants us to possess the land. He will use the enemy's rejection to open your eyes to the blessing that will make rich and add no sorrow with it.

It is important to only want what God ordains for your life because it means you don't desire to have someone else's stuff. You could be hindering someone's blessing or miracle and they could be hindering yours. The sooner that man rejects you the sooner you can move on to the one God really has for you. The sooner those saints reject you as pastor, the sooner God can send the hundreds to replace them, the sooner the better. As painful as it may seem, this cross will lead to life. This is why Jesus said to Judas;

St. John 13:27 *"That thou doest, do quickly"*

Sometimes we try to avoid the inevitable instead of accepting and confronting the issue at hand. We try to hold on to what we know is going to leave us anyway. Jesus didn't do that. He knew Satan had entered Judas and there was no use in trying to stop him or talk him out of this betrayal. Jesus wanted it over and done with so he could gather in the multitude of souls both Jew and Gentile who would eventually become heirs of God and joint-heirs with him. Once Judas was out of the way, the other eleven apostles could choose his replacement. The Holy Ghost could fall and they could turn the world upside down. If he isn't going to marry you then you want him to go ahead and reject you so you can move on to who the Lord has for you. It may be painful, but let him do it quickly. Don't chase him because that is not the order of God. The man should find you because you're the good thing and you cause him to experience favor. You may cry when he walks out but it is best that he does it before you marry him, rather than three years into the marriage. Let him do it now. Go through it because I guarantee you God has something better on his mind for you. If they don't hurry up and get out of the way, God can't give it to you.

I John 2:19 (The Message) *"They left us, but they were never really with us. If they had been, they would have stuck it out with us, loyal to the end. In leaving, they showed their true colors, showed they never did belong."*

Too often we make the mistake of crying over spilled milk. It is the will of God which must again become the most important thing to us. The things I want and the things other people want for me are not the most important thing. The most important thing is what my heavenly Father wants for me. Because if I don't do his will, I will not live forever.

> I John 2:17 *"...but he that doeth the will of God abideth forever."*

As long as we deny ourselves for the will of God we will remain focused and strong. It is those who try to save their lives who will lose their lives, but those who lose their lives will save their lives. We must understand that the Lord has searched us out before we arrived on this planet. He knows us. God knows our down sitting and our uprising as well as our thoughts afar off. We need only what he brings our way. We must rest in the fact that what hasn't and who hasn't been ordained for us, can't stay with us. Our peace is lost if we try to order our own steps. We must remind ourselves that God has fashioned us. He has ordained us to be productive men and women of God. We can't be that way holding on to unproductive people and things. God has precious thoughts about us and those who He has ordained for our lives will also allow precious thoughts about us to govern their thought life.

The rejection purges you from seasonal stuff to receive the eternal things the Father has ordained. You may cry about something that was seasonal, but you will laugh about the things that are eternal. As you refocus on doing God's will, you will understand why your prayers couldn't hold this person in your life and neither could your fasting. It will become clearer to you as you understand you are in this race to please the one who called you, who is God. Remember, you are dead to your will and you are alive to His. You will thank Him through tears now, but later you will thank Him through a smile as time unfolds His good, acceptable, and perfect will for your life.

The rejection helps you remain dead to your own agenda. People around you will say, "I wouldn't take that if I were you." They will try to make you feel stupid or less than who God has made you to be. Notice these words,

> St. Luke 23:35 *"And the people stood beholding.*
> *And the rulers also with them derided him, saying,*
> *He saved others; let him save himself, if he be*
> *Christ, the chosen of God."*

Notice Jesus never responded or acted to these words, because he wanted the will of God to be done in his life. He counted not his own life dear unto himself. He never allowed the rejection to cause him to pick his life back up. He laid it down and it stayed laid down. We must do the same because our lives are not our own. We must listen to those who are crucified with Christ and don't listen to those who are not.

True happiness is only found by those who are walking in the perfect will of God for their lives. The rejection you may feel is nothing compared to getting something or someone who moves you out of the will of God. This will cause death to your spirit. Your inner man will be miserable when you chose something against God's plan and purpose for your life.

Moses chose to suffer with God's people rather than to enjoy the pleasures of sin for a season. He had all kinds of riches in Egypt, but he walked away from it all in order to be in the perfect will of God. You may have to walk away from some glamorous things in order to live in the will of God. Paul walked away from his Jewish roots and counted it as dung for the excellence of Christ. He wanted to do the will of God.

Sometimes, you can't always tell what it is God wants you to have. This is when God will step in and eliminate choices for you. He will give you uneasiness in your spirit or allow you to be turned down for something He doesn't want you to have. God will not let certain things work out if you don't override His will for your life. He will allow you to see certain negative qualities about an individual if He knows you are sincere about doing His will. God will let you see things that will cause you to end the whole relationship because He knows your future. You must not put anybody or anything before the will of God.

#7
MOVES YOU FROM CHRONOS TO KAIROS

One of the greatest gifts given to man by God is time. However, most people are asking the question, "where is all my time going or where has all my time gone?" This question is due to the fact that most of us are living in the chronos of time, but few are living in the kairos of time. **Chronos** deals with the ordinary days, months, and years we live here on earth. **Kairos** deals with the significant moments in life. It is the meeting of natural time with destiny. The kairos of time is the place where great memories occur. This type of time sets you up for God's favor. It sets history into motion. It is the place of the unforgettable! These moments of kairos offer refreshing to your spirit, soul and body. They cause you to live and experience life on a whole new level.

Rejection realigns your whole course in life. It puts you on schedule with the right people, in the right place at the right time. Moses, who fled from the face of Pharaoh into the land of Midian, sat down by a well. He didn't know that Jethro, who was a priest of Midian, had seven daughters, nor did he know that they would come to draw water from the same well he sat by. Moses had to defend Jethro's daughters from the shepherds who came and drove them away. Jethro heard about what Moses did for his daughter and called him to eat. Moses was content to dwell with him, but God took this moment in time to set Moses up with Jethro's daughter named Zipporah. The rest is history.

It is also important to note that the adversary is holding somebody up until you arrive at your kairos in time. The daughters of Jethro were always arriving back home later than they were suppose to because the shepherds held them up.

Exodus 2:18 *"And when they came to Reuel their father, he said, How is it that ye are come so soon to day?"*

This verse leads us to know that because of the help of Moses, the daughters arrived home at an earlier time. So many people are waiting on you to get in place so they can experience their kairos moment. The enemy is trying to keep them away from the Well of Living Water. You and I must be in position to fight off the enemy, so they are not held up any longer.

Jesus sat by the well and invited the woman at the well into a kairos moment. She was use to going to the well and returning back to her same routine, but this time things would be different. Jesus ministered to her in such a way that it caused her to leave her waterpot and forget about the natural water she went to the well to get. It was a life changing moment for her.

St. John 4:28,29 *"The woman then left her waterpot, and went her way into the city, and saith to the men, Come, see a man, which told me all the things that ever I did: is not this the Christ?"*

This moment was very powerful for her. She began to desire others to come and see him. She wanted them to know she had found the Christ. The daily routines of life are broken when we meet with destiny. It calls us out of time into eternity where we experience God in a way that causes us to leave negative behavior behind.

You've got to move from the familiar into the unknown because God has interrupted my dull, dry schedule with His exciting new one. The eternal things of God seem more real to you than the temporal things of man. This is when you will really start to seem crazy to some people. One day they saw you all calm and seemingly uninterested in life and suddenly you are vibrant and full of zest for life. It's because the rejection ran you into your due season. The word **Zipporah** means "bird." You and I must believe that God is removing those people and things from us that are holding us down and connecting us to those people and things that will cause us to take flight or fly as a bird. The rejection is getting the things out of your life that have tried to weigh you down. You are about to take flight and soar to places in God you have never been before. The free favors of God will abound in your life and you will not look back with any remorse.

Luke 4:19 *"To preach the acceptable year of the Lord."*

St. Luke 4:19 (Amplified) *"To proclaim the accepted and acceptable year of the Lord [the day when salvation and the free favors of God profusely abound."*

Most great men and women of God have walked with God long enough to almost tell when something great is about to happen. If you talk to them, they will clue you in on the fact that right before the set time or kairos moment, is a battle with the adversary. The rejection is a sign that your kairos moment is near. Something eternal will always cause something in the temporal to shift, so we must expect the powers of darkness to act up. Don't allow whining or fear to cause someone else to experience kairos moments and you only stand back and hear about them.

Jesus didn't step into his kairos moment in preaching until John was put in prison.

St. Mark 1:14,15 *"Now after that John was put in prison, Jesus came into Galilee, preaching the*

*gospel of the kingdom of God, And saying, The
time is fulfilled, and the kingdom of God is at hand:
repent ye, and believe the gospel."*

Jesus didn't cry for John nor weep for John because he knew John's season was over. It was time for Jesus to go forth then. Now it is your time. It's your time to be blessed. It's your time to be healed and appreciated. You can't sit back and act pitiful or complain about how people have treated you. It's your time to speak a relevant word to those who are in need of hearing the gospel.

God will challenge you to inconvenience yourself for him so that he can bring you into your kairos moment. You can't afford to say, "God, I'll go after I get over what people said or did to me." You have to know how to bring healing to people while you're being crucified. This is what makes your kairos moment so special to you because you walked through the valley and shadow of death to get to it. The rejection will make it look and feel as if you are moving further and further away from the ordained time. It will seem as if everything God told you is a lie, but don't be deceived. You will see a sudden move of God that will turn everything around! It will happen quickly and without any warning, so I challenge you to stay ready. Your kairos moment will shake your enemies up. It will cause those who expected you to die to be flabbergasted by this sudden door of increase God sends your way.

Another good example of the kairos moment is found in the book of II Kings the eighth chapter. God used the prophet Elisha to tell a woman whose son he had restored to life to sojourn wheresoever she could for seven years because the Lord had called for a famine. This woman obeyed the prophet and sojourned in the land of the Philistines, but at the end of the seven years she returned out of the land to cry out unto the king for her house and her land. The king was talking to Gehazi, the servant of Elisha, to hear all the great things the man of God had done. It came to pass, as he was telling the king how Elisha had restored a dead body to life, that the woman, whose son he had restored came in and cried unto the king. Gehazi was startled. He said, "My lord, O king, this is the woman, and this is her son, whom Elisha restored to life." The next verse states something that is absolutely incredible.

> II Kings 8:6 *"And when the king asked the woman, she told him. So the king appointed unto her a certain officer, saying, Restore all that was hers, and all the fruits of the field since the day that she left the land, even until now."*

This verse shows us how God will set us up for total restoration by a kairos moment. He allowed this woman to come in the presence of the king at the exact time the servant of Elisha was talking about her and her son. She was rewarded for those bad years or years of famine also. Her divine moment brought her to a bigger and better place in life. God caused her to forget the toil in her life.

This is exactly what happened to Joseph after he endured his period of rejection. Joseph called the name of his first-born **Manasseh** which means, "God hath made me forget all my toil, and all my father's house." The God we serve orchestrated a kairos moment because only Joseph was able to reveal Pharaoh's secrets or reveal Pharaoh's dreams. This kairos moment led Joseph, as well as the woman in the book of Kings into their due season. It may appear to you that the rejection is moving you further away from your due season, but God whose ways are so deep is leading you right into it.

As we live for God's glory, we know that God will make everything beautiful in His time. He set Moses up with the priest of Midian. God will bring you across a person empowered by Him with the things you need. Moses needed a place to stay and he needed a wife or a woman to help him. He needed someone to give him proper training in the caring of sheep. God knew what Moses didn't know. He knew Moses was ordained to lead Israel out of bondage. Moses was about to experience the best days of his life and he didn't have a clue. Everything that had caused his parents to hide him when he was young was about to manifest itself in his life.

The kairos moment brings you in contact with people who not only can help you but those who you can help. It will never bring you into one-sided relationships. You will be thankful you met them and they will be thankful they met you. You will appreciate the fact that God brought them in your life when he did. You both will know it wasn't coincidental, but a divine set up. You will value the relationship because it came at a time when others didn't believe in you or couldn't see the true greatness God had in your life. The relationship is precious because the prophetic clock of eternity caused this connection to happen.

These relationships bring about redemption for you and others. They will cause you to forget the negative experiences you've had with others who didn't value you. You will understand this kairos moment wouldn't have occurred if the rejection hadn't occurred first. You are hungry for real relationship and so are they. You have no wrong motives and neither do they. The process of time has you desiring to make an impact in the kingdom of God. Everything about your life will now go down in history!

These moments will leave a mark on your family and environment that will never be forgotten. Your life will be forever branded on the canvas of your family's mind. They will be discussing how God delivered you at the supper table many years after you're gone. They will be discussing your deliverance with your children's children. They will know that God brought you out with his own right hand. Yes, his own right arm hath gotten him the victory in your life.

Your kairos moment will be used as a shield of faith and confidence for your family in the years to come. They will face the future knowing the same God who showed you miraculous things will do the same thing for them. As they discuss your legacy, they will be proud of your walk of faith. Through faith you will know all things are possible and great things await you in this season of your life.

#8
BRINGS PROMOTION

The eighth blessing of rejection is knowing that it brings promotion. Promotion comes in an unidentifiable package called rejection. It is knowing this which will cause you to be a steadfast, unmovable believer.

Psalms 118:23 *"The stone which the builders refused is become the head stone of the corner. This is the Lord's doing; it is marvelous in our eyes. This is the day which the Lord hath made; we will rejoice and be glad in it."*

The psalmist who speaks prophetically about Jesus Christ understands the process. He is well aware that Jesus will receive a name above every name once the rejection is over. God delights in lifting up the down trodden. He will always bring about promotion after you've endured hardness as a good soldier. Promotion from God is an awesome thing because people can't take the credit for where he has taken you.

The Jews rejected Jesus. Joseph's brothers rejected him and Moses' brothers rejected him. But the God we serve, promoted all three men. He raised them up from the bottom to the top. They didn't allow the rejection to take their eyes off the call of God upon their lives. They trusted the fact that God was with them. Carnal minded brothers rejected them, but God promoted them. Their brothers were too familiar with them. They only saw them in the natural, but God wanted them to be seen in the spiritual. We must remember God knows who you are in the spirit. The word of God has already declared that you are the head and not the tail. This means promotion will manifest in the natural world because it has already been established in the spirit world. Those who are spiritual are not judging you according to the flesh. They believe in the anointing of God and the change God has made in your life.

> II Corinthians 5:16 *"Wherefore henceforth know we no man after the flesh: yea though we have known Christ after the flesh, yet now henceforth know we him no more."*

Based on this scripture, we should know Jesus today as the Apostle and high priest of our profession. Our focus must not only deal with who he was when he walked this earth, but who he is now. Today, he lives as an intercessor for us. Jesus is now able to be touched with the feeling of our infirmities or weaknesses. He is to be viewed in the spirit.

In the spirit everything takes on a greater glory than it appears to have in the natural. This is why Paul wasn't seeking to know any man after the flesh, but after the spirit. He knew the flesh limits you and weakens who you truly are. Those who view you after the spirit understand the might on the inside of you. They understand you are a new creature in Christ with the ability to bring about reformation. Jesus, Moses, and Joseph brought reformation to their world. We can do the same after we have walked through the fires of rejection.

God promotes because he doesn't see selfishness. The promotion given to you by God is never to cause us to look down on others who are in despair. It is given to help others experience liberation. The promotion will not only be marvelous in your eyes, but in the eyes of others. You know what it feels like to be rejected and you go forth looking to lift up others. Your promotion doesn't bring pain and sorrow to others, but it causes them to experience joy. Others acknowledge the hand of God on your life. They know God raised you up to be a blessing. Every great man and woman of God

I know is not preaching for the things. They have things, but things don't have them. They have a sincere desire to help people. It is all about how many people we can help. We must help those on drugs, bad marriages, wayward children, raped victims, and violent teens. Whenever those who have been rejected meet hurting individuals, they strive to help them. God will always give his best to those who care about others. Those who aren't saved or those who aren't walking close with God will try to make it look like it's about the things. It is not. The things are added because we desire to help those Jesus died for.

St. Matthew 6:33 *"Seek ye first the kingdom of God, and his righteousness; and all these things shall be added unto you."*

The more you desire to help others the more you will receive from God and the bigger the promotion will be from him. The information the Heavenly Father has given you is not to be used to show off, but it is to be used to empower others with the knowledge. There are many vessels who have a wrong motive but they are usually those who haven't been through the fire of rejection. They haven't been through what it takes to burn those type of ropes off their hands. On the other hand, there are those being used around the world today whose only desire is to exalt Christ and those who are cast down.

God, who knows the heart, will promote you after you've been rejected. This promotion can't be rushed or manipulated. It is coming!

Psalm 75:6,7 *"For promotion cometh neither from the east, not from the west, nor from the south. But God is the judge: he putteth down one, and setteth up another."*

This is where your faith in God must be exercised. You must boldly confess your promotion to yourself. You must speak it so loud to yourself that it drowns out the rejection being tossed your way. Notice, I didn't say you have to speak it to others, but you must speak it to yourself. This will help you stay encouraged about the promotion God is bringing your way. You must be convinced that those who have exalted themselves will be brought low and those who are at the bottom will be brought to the top. You may have been overlooked by man, but you have not been overlooked by God. Speak to yourself about your promotion in the face of trials and tests. Speak to yourself about your promotion that God has for you while you're in prison or in the lion's den of life.

Jesus spoke constantly about his promotion. He knew if they destroyed his temple, the Father would raise him back up again. This caused him to live a committed life toward the Father. Many times we aren't trusting God to promote us and it shows in our level of commitment. There is no way you can tell me you expect God to bring promotion in your life and you rarely go to the house of God. You can't tell me you expect God to promote you and you refuse to tithe and give appropriate offerings. You can't tell me you expect God to promote you and you don't strive to live a holy life.

You are committed to who you believe holds your increase. Football, baseball, and basketball players demonstrate commitment to their teams. We must be committed to God and his kingdom. He promotes the faithful and faithfulness is proven during times of rejection. Anybody can be faithful while things are pleasant. But when you are being scoffed at or mocked; can you still be faithful?

I Corinthians 4:2 *"Moreover it is required in stewards, that a man be found faithful."*

The apostle Paul is speaking in this verse about being faithful as ministers with the mysteries of God. He is causing us to know that God has trusted us with his secret purposes and we must take it seriously. Even under extreme pressure Paul stayed faithful. He never swayed or strayed from the assignment given to him by God. He was faithful when he looked like a fool for Christ. He was faithful when he was despised and felt weak. He was faithful while being defamed and reviled. He was faithful in the midst of those who made him feel like the filth of the world. I believe Paul knew he had to be a model of faithfulness for his son in the gospel, Timothy, and others who would follow after him. We must do the same. We must make it clear to others that we will be faithful no matter what.

I Corinthians 4:2 New Century Version says,
"Those who are trusted with something valuable must show they are worthy of that trust."

We must once again acknowledge that God gave us valuable stuff. We are in charge of things that the enemy would love to get from us. These mysteries pull the devil's authority down. We must comprehend that as we are faithful over a few things, God will make us a ruler over many things. We are on our way toward bigger and better things and God (who we are striving to please) is watching us and ready to promote his sons and daughters. We must continue to do what we are doing heartily unto the Lord, knowing our reward is coming from him.

Colossians 3:23,24 *"And whatsoever ye do, do it heartily, as to the Lord, and not unto men: Knowing that of the Lord ye shall receive the reward of the inheritance: for ye serve the Lord Christ.*

We are not men pleasers. We are God pleasers. We are doing his will with everything in us. It is not our goal or desire to be seen of men, but rather to be seen by God. We are doing God's will from the heart to be rewarded by him.

Ephesians 6:6-8 *"Not with eye service, as men pleasers; but as the servants of Christ, doing the will of God from the heart; With good will doing service, as to the Lord, and not to men: Knowing that whatsoever good thing any man doeth the same shall he receive of the Lord, whether he be bond or free."*

The church or the called out believers understand we can only render to God the type of service he deserves and needs in singleness of motive. We are eager and ready to please him. We love him and we are prepared to be exalted by him!

Proverbs 28:20 *"The faithful man shall abound in blessings: but he that maketh haste to be rich shall not be innocent."*

The Message Translation says, *"Committed and persistent work pays off, get rich-quick schemes are ripoffs."*

Those who expect God to bless them are not trying to get rich in a hurry, we recognize God's way takes time. We understand that this promotion that comes from him will not be a hasty promotion, but it will come in the process of time. We are willing to stay the course for the long haul and we are looking to God. He will bring forth faithful servants everywhere. We will keep looking until we see something about the size of a man's hand. Though it doesn't seem like much it will contain the abundance of rain we need to bring us out of our dilemma. This abundance of rain will make up for all of the dry years in your life. No matter how long the wait we must concentrate on hearing the sound of the abundance of rain. A lot of the members in the body of Christ become so focus on what they see that they fail to listen. The Bible teaches us that faith comes by hearing, not by seeing. So if you are going by what you see, rather than what you are hearing, you are going to miss the rain every time. You must listen to the word of faith being preached more than the circumstance the devil is showing you. The sound that is being echoed across the pulpit each Sunday cannot be taken lightly. Everybody can't hear it and those of us who hear it must be prepared to get up on our feet because rain is right around the corner.

I remember as a child growing up watching the Andy Griffith Show. It is still one of my favorite shows today in syndication. I love the episode that Barney is trying to train this particular dog. The dog was named "Blue." The dog never responded to any of Barney's commands. Yet, when Barney took out a whistle from his shirt pocket the dog arose and went into an attack mode. Neither Barney nor Andy could hear the whistle, but Blue could hear it. Because of the dogs ability to hear the sound of the whistle a criminal was captured at the end of the episode. The dog that acted slow and uninterested would arise and bark once anyone blew the whistle.

Those of us who are saved are hearing a sound that the world isn't hearing. It is forecasting rain for you and I. It is challenging us to pounce on the enemy the same way Blue rose up in the Andy Griffith Show. The whistle of the Spirit is blowing and those who hear it will take charge.

The sound will not lie to you. It announces that overflow is on its way. So, get ready to celebrate!

I Kings 18:41 *"And Elijah said unto Ahab, Get thee up, eat and drink; for there is a sound of abundance of rain."*

The Message Translation says, *"Elijah said to Ahab, "Up on your feet! Eat and drink—celebrate! Rain is on the way, I hear it coming."*

#9
GIVES YOU A CHANCE TO THANK THOSE WHO
HELPED YOU ALONG THE WAY

God is good and His mercy endureth forever seems to always be a praise given by those who had to walk through periods of rejection. We are willing to acknowledge him with our praise and we must appreciate others who played a role in the victory we've seen in our lives. Those who came with words of kindness and grace, those who refused to let us die with our dreams still inside of us, and those who held our hand and walked with us through the dry places, deserve to be recognized.

We must have an attitude of gratitude towards those who loved us enough to make an investment into our future. Their deposit can never be taken for granted. The apostle Paul always thanked and acknowledged those who assisted him in ministry. He challenged the saints to salute and greet many of the saints who were helpful in the success he experienced in ministry.

> Romans 16:3,4 *"Greet Priscilla and Aquila my helpers in Christ Jesus: Who have for my life laid down their own necks: unto whom not only I give thanks, but also all the churches of the Gentiles."*

In the sixteenth chapter of Romans, not only did Paul thank these two vessels for their support, but he saluted many others. There are always others who are laying their lives on the line to help you achieve. Their help is so vital to the advancement of the kingdom of God. It may go unnoticed by others, but it should never go unnoticed by you. The man or woman of God seen out front has help in the background. In any song that becomes a hit, if you don't have good background singers the song wouldn't sound as good. The harmony of the singers in the background has to be almost perfect. They have to sound like one voice. The person who is singing the solo may be known by name, but the background singers play a significant role in the sale of the song.

The same is true in the movies. The actors who receive their awards always thank the other actors in the film. They acknowledge them, their producers, and directors even though those watching the film may not acknowledge them. The body of Christ sometimes fail to give credit to the background. This is why some push and shove to be out front. We must comprehend the fact that the person out front couldn't achieve at the level he or she does without the assistance of others in the background.

As I hear the background singers I become more appreciative of their skill level. I recognize they are using what God has given them to help another person shine. We must appreciate those who have used the gifts of helps to help great leaders accomplish great things. Even though others want to constantly acknowledge us as leaders; we should constantly acknowledge and exalt others.

Philippians 2:3,4 *"Let nothing be done through strife or vainglory; but in lowliness of mind let each esteem other better than themselves. Look not every man on his own things, but every man also on the things of others."*

The Message Translation says, *"Agree with each other, be deep-spirited friends. Don't push your way to the front; don't sweet-talk your way to the top. Put yourself aside, and help others get ahead. Don't be obsessed with getting your own advantage. Forget yourselves long enough to lend a helping hand."*

We must acknowledge our spouses, parents, elders, ministers, deacons, congregations and partners. These people have played a significant part in advancing the kingdom of God. Their prayers, finances, and very presence has helped to bring to pass the corporate vision God has given to the leaders we see out front today.

Jesus, who is our ultimate example didn't fail to acknowledge and appreciate his help. Even though Jesus was anointed with the Holy Spirit, he still needed anointed help. The disciples were a great asset to the ministry of Jesus Christ.

> St. Luke 22:28-30 *"Ye are they which have continued with me in my temptations. And I appoint unto you a kingdom, as my Father hath appointed unto me; That ye may eat and drink at my table in my kingdom, and sit on thrones judging the twelve tribes of Israel."*

Jesus knew he wasn't always appreciated and valued by everyone, yet the disciples had done their very best to stand by his side. They had endured a lot for the name of Jesus. Walking with Jesus made them go through pain and turmoil, but it also brought them to blessings promised by our Lord.

Men and women of God who are on the frontline will be controversial. They will be praised by some and ridiculed by others. In the midst of their battles we must continue to walk with them in an assurance that God will sustain them through their temptations.

Those who stand with them will be appreciated by them and will experience an exaltation from God. Let's stand with the righteous!

> Hebrews 6:10 *"For God is not unrighteous to forget your work and labour of love, which ye have shown*

toward his name, in that ye have ministered to the
saints, and do minister."

This verse admonishes us that when we demonstrate love towards the saints that we are showing love toward God's name. It also tells us that God will never forget what you and I do in ministering to the saints. This means that God sees his people as his prize possession. He wants us to work together as one man.

Psalms 133:1 *"Behold, how good and how pleasant*
it is for brethren to dwell together in unity."

The Message Translation says, *"How wonderful,*
how beautiful, when brothers and sisters get along!

Judges 20:11 *"So all the men of Israel were gath-*
ered against the city, knit together as one man."

#10
CAUSES YOU TO IMPROVISE

One of the most exciting things about being rejected is that you will begin to use what you have been given by God. Every time you consult him about what has to be done, God will remind you of what you have in your hand. He will not allow you to look at what you don't have. He wants you to see his glory revealed as you put to use those things and people currently around you. Moses was giving God all kinds of excuses why he couldn't face Pharoah, but none of the excuses were addressed by God. He only prompted Moses to use what he had in his hand.

Exodus 4:1-3 *"And Moses answered and said, But, behold, they will not believe me, nor hearken unto my voice: for they will say, The Lord hath not appeared unto thee. And the Lord said unto him, What is that in thine hand? And he said, A rod. And he said, Cast it on the ground. And he cast it on the ground, and it became a serpent; and Moses fled from before it. And the Lord said unto Moses, Put forth thine hand, and take it by the tail. And he put forth his hand, and caught it, and it became a rod in his hand."*

We can see based on these verses that he was afraid of the rejection he would receive from his brethren. He feared they wouldn't believe God had sent him. The Lord showed Moses that He is able to take what we have and cause great things to be manifested. As Moses cast the rod to the ground it became something totally different. We have to take what God has given us and use it. As we cast it down, it will become something usable to swallow up the devil's attack against us.

The day of being one-dimensional is over. You and I must be flexible enough to adjust to the situations at hand without breaking. This is why God puts new wine in new wineskins. We have to be able to stretch as the challenges of life come our way. As companies close down and file for bankruptcy many people are finding themselves having to go back to school or do something totally different from what they've grown accustomed to. The only way to keep up with an ever changing society is to be able to improvise. A person who knows how to improvise effectively will never be beaten. Mainly, because they know how to make the most out of a bad situation. The word **improvise** means, "to make for the occasion, to make up something on the spur of the moment, or to speak without preparation." This is exactly what God is showing Moses that He is able to do. This is why God will always be triumphant, because He is the I AM THAT I AM. God can become anything we need at any given moment. God showed Moses that He could even turn his hand white with leprosy and then turn it back to normal again.

> Exodus 4:6,7 *"And the Lord said furthermore unto him, Put forth thine hand, into thy bosom. And he put his hand into his bosom: and when he took it out, behold, his hand was leprous as snow. And he said, Put thine hand into thy bosom again. And he put his hand into his bosom again; and plucked it out of his bosom, and, behold, it was turned again as his other flesh."*

Rejection requires us to be able to do things at a spur of the moment. Suppose you had several key members leave your church in one day without any advanced noticed. Dr. I. V. Hillard gives his testimony frequently about how his congregation went from 300 members to 23 members as he followed the voice of God concerning the kingdom of God.

No doubt he had to be able to improvise in the midst of rejection. Thank God he did and the rest is history!

I remember getting ready to begin our morning worship service years ago, when my wife and I were told by the musician and his wife that they were leaving the church. We had been very generous and patient with this couple on many occasions, yet this is the thanks leaders get for their servitude. They didn't tell us two weeks before the service, but they told us ten minutes before the service began. My wife and I never worried nor did we shed a tear. We knew we had to explain it to the congregation and move on in Jesus name. We told them that we were going on and God was going to do everything he had promised to do for us. My wife played and sang. I helped lead the saints in worship, preached and the anointing of God did the rest. God stepped in and the next thing I knew we were given favor to go on television. Praise be unto God!

I can recall another situation in Dillon, South Carolina. A great apostle friend and mentor of mine was conducting a leadership conference. People were present from many different parts and places of the world. He and his wife were speaking tremendous truths and insights into the hearts and minds of the leaders present. The man of God had just been given a powerful prophetic word by another great man of God by the name of Kelly Varner. As Apostle Michael Goings was about to approach the pulpit to continue to speak to the leaders in the second half of the conference, a note was handed to him. The note was a resignation letter from some of their key leaders in ministry. He preached and flowed in the anointing in spite of this type of rejection being thrown at him in the midst of a leadership conference where others were being strengthened. God will bring forth the ability to improvise in your life and show you his glory in these types of situations.

Elisha was called upon to help a woman and her sons get out of debt. Her sons were about to be taken as slaves by the creditor. The woman didn't recognize that she had the ability to experience a notable miracle as she improvised. She didn't know what God was about to do with the pot of oil she had. Elisha told her to go, borrow empty vessels from all the neighbors. He told her to borrow not a few. She was then advised to go in and shut the door upon her and her sons, and pour out the oil in all the vessels. The oil didn't stop until there were no more empty vessels. Then the man of God told her to go, sell the oil, pay her debt and live off the rest (II Kings 4:1-7).

This woman had never sold oil before, but the situation demanded that she improvise. She had to do something she wasn't use to doing. The deliverance the woman needed was in her ability to improvise. The rejections of life will cause you to hear the prophetic word and act on it. The Lord will cause you to hear a word that will cause you to pay attention to something you've overlooked. He will cause you to use insignificant things to get significant things done. God will also cause you to speak without preparation. He will give you and I divine wisdom and words which are unrehearsed. The Holy Spirit will give us divine utterances that will confound those around us. He knows how to minister to those in your home and on your job. We must look and expect these supernatural thoughts and ideas to be given to us. As these thoughts come, we must not be afraid to speak them and act in faith upon them. Remember these thoughts will always be validated by the written word.

Our great grandparents and grandparents survived and overcame by their ability to improvise. They took a banana, bread, and mayonnaise and created a banana sandwich. They took bread and molasses and created a sandwich. They took crackers and mayonnaise and created something to eat. They knew how to improvise. Even when they didn't have money to buy the kind of toys they needed, they improvised. They took rocks and a small ball and played jacks. They took a piece of broken glass and drew squares in the dirt and played hopscotch. They took an old extension cord or anything similar to a rope and played jump rope. They took a tobacco stick and rode on it like it was a horse. They never allowed themselves to make excuses about their lack. Their ability to improvise compensated for everything they didn't seem to have.

This is what sowing and reaping says to us. God never expects a man to give what he doesn't have. He expects us to give according to our ability and He will multiply the seed that we sow. The widow woman of Zarephath was expecting to eat one last meal with her son and die. However, the prophet Elijah was told by God to go to her. God told him that he had commanded her to sustain him. In the natural she didn't have enough to sustain herself, but the prophet told her to make him a little cake first, and after make for her and her son. He told her the barrel of meal would not waste, neither the cruse of oil fail, until the day that the Lord sendeth rain upon the earth. She did what the man of God said and they all ate many days (I Kings 17:8-15).

It is the adversary's job to blind the minds of those who are not saved. He doesn't want them to see the light. But he will also try to blind the believer to what we currently possess that will dispel the darkness around us. Jesus took the little lad's two fish and five loaves of bread in order to feed five thousand men. He didn't send the people away to the marketplace. Instead, he told the disciples to make the people sit down. He took what he had and gave thanks to the Father. He blessed it and gave it to the disciples. They gave it to the people and they did all eat and were filled.

Jesus also improvised when he had told his disciples to pass over to the other side. He had no boat to travel in and no one was going that way any time soon, so he walked on water. He wasn't doing this to show off, because that wasn't the nature of Jesus. He did it because he had to improvise. He had to use what he had at his disposal. He had to walk on water. He had no other choice. Some of us have no other choice, but to improvise or die. And we refuse to die with this mighty God inside of us. We must not allow anyone to cause us to underestimate what we have. We must believe the words of the apostle Paul,

Ephesians 3:20 *"Now unto him which is able to do exceeding abundantly above all that we ask or think, according to the power that worketh in us."*

The Message Translation says, *"God can do anything, you know—far more than you could ever imagine or guess or request in your wildest dreams! He does it not by pushing us around but by working within us, his Spirit deeply and gently within us."*

Most of the time we never see what God can do because we wait until all the conditions are right. This will always keep you from achieving because those of us who see the miraculous have to trust God when things look unfavorable. Jesus had disciples who suggested sending the multitude away because they thought the multitude would faint after following Jesus three days without food. However, Jesus told his disciples to make them sit down in companies of fifty. Jesus took the little lad's two fish and five loaves of bread and fed five thousand men not including women and children. He showed his disciples how to improvise.

This is one of the reasons I like the movie "Rambo (First Blood)." We are able to see a warrior who knew how to live off the land and eat stuff that would make a Billy goat puke. The Colonel told the forest rangers and police force that Rambo had seen every possible thing that they could throw at him. He told them that he didn't come to save Rambo from them, but he came to save them from Rambo. The Colonel knew he had trained Rambo to survive.

Many of us in the Body of Christ attend Bible study, conferences, and Sunday morning worship services, yet when we have to improvise we act like we don't know what to do. We can't allow the situations of life to shut down our ability to think in line with the word of God. God has the power to take what we present to him and stretch it. He will cause multiplication to take place.

Our knowledge of this causes us to function without any excuses. We don't care what we have or don't have we believe God can do what he said. We believe God will take small things and make big things happen. He will take the unknowns to confound those who are known. He is just looking for those who will get rid of every excuse and use what they have.

#11
CAUSES US NOT TO BE IMPRESSED WITH THE FLESH

The rejection of your life will cause you to think soberly about yourself and others. It will cause you to stop making idols of men. You will start to recognize that you are to honor and respect men, but not worship men. Peter and Paul never allowed men or women to worship them. Because of the power of God moving in their lives they challenged men to know that they weren't gods, but men used by the Holy Spirit. Once you've been rejected you will understand that you don't have to be impressed with anyone but God. You will stop viewing anointed men and women as movie stars and celebrities. You will understand that God has an expectation of everyone of His children and He is no respecter of persons. God wants us to reverence Him and believe in the authority He has given us as believers in Jesus Christ.

Because so many of us in the body of Christ aren't using this authority we have allowed ourselves to stand gazing at those who are using their authority. Instead, we need to stir ourselves to work the works of Jesus while it is day.

St John 14:12 *"Verily, verily, I say unto you. He that believeth on me, the works that I do shall he do also; and greater works than these shall he do because I go unto my Father."*

St. Mark 16:17,18 *"And these signs shall follow them that believe: In my name shall they cast out devils; they shall speak with new tongues; They shall take up serpents; and if they drink any deadly thing, it shall not hurt them; they shall lay hands on the sick, and they shall recover."*

We are the sons of God and everyone of us have to believe these verses of scriptures. We must stop believing that the apostle, prophet, evangelist, pastor, and teacher can lay hands on the sick, but you can't. You have to know that these ministry gifts are preaching, teaching, and declaring God's word to you so you can do the work of the ministry.

> Ephesians 4:11,12 *"And he gave some, apostles; and some, prophets, and some, evangelists; and some, pastors and teachers; For the perfecting of the saints, for the work of the ministry, for the edifying of the body of Christ."*

The believer must understand that the Lord has given him power to revolutionize his life as well as the lives of others. He has been equipped to pray for himself and bring hope to those in despair. I've seen so many believers act as if they have little or no faith in their own prayers. They seem to have more faith in the prayers of well known leaders than they do their own. The truth of the matter is that God will hear your prayers the same way He will your Bishop's prayer. The blood of Jesus made this possible. The blood has given us access to the Father. This word **access** in the Greek language literally means a "private and personal interview." The blood rent (tore) the veil and made available to us an up close conversation with our Heavenly Father. Now we must ask in his name and according to his will and he will hear us. We must believe that since he hears us; we will receive those things we have desired of him.

Many leaders who haven't experienced the fires of life are still impressed with themselves and others. They are still chasing the flesh and not the word of God. Once the ark of the covenant which was carried by the priest moved the children of Israel were told to go after it. They weren't told to go after them (the priests), but after it (the ark) which symbolizes Jesus Christ and the word of God.

> Joshua 3:3,4 *"And they commanded the people, saying, When ye see the ark of the covenant of the Lord your God, and the priests the Levites bearing it, then ye shall remove from your place, and go after it. Yet there shall be a space between you and it, about two thousand cubits by measure: come not near unto it, that ye may know the way by which ye must go: for ye have not passed this way before."*

We must pursue obeying the Lord and his word. We must be fully persuaded that doing the word of God is the only thing that offers us true deliverance. The doers of the word are blessed.

> James 1:22,25 *"But be ye doers of the word, and not hearers only, deceiving your own selves. But whoso looketh into the perfect law of liberty, and continueth therein, he being not a forgetful hearer, but a doer of the work, this man shall be blessed in his deed."*

> The Amplified says, *"But be doers of the Word [obey the message], and not merely listeners to it betraying yourselves [into deception by reasoning contrary to the Truth]. But he who looks carefully into the faultless law, the [law] of liberty, and is faithful to it and perseveres in looking into it, being not a heedless listener who forgets but an active doer [who obeys], he shall be blessed in his doing (his life of obedience)."*

The Message Translation says, *"Don't fool yourself into thinking that you are a listener when
you are anything but, letting the Word go in one
ear and out the other. Act on what you hear! But
whoever catches a glimpse of the revealed counsel
of God—the free life!—even out of the corner of his
eye, and sticks with it, is no distracted scatterbrain
but a man or woman of action. That person will find
delight and affirmation in the action."*

The word of God must impress us and not flesh. The word of God is the thing that will bring us into the liberty of God. It is the thing that is alive and will never die. Men and women of God will eventually die. They will not live and abide in their temporal bodies forever.

Also, notice the officers told the people to not come near it (the ark). They were told to leave a space of about 2,000 cubits. This is God's way of admonishing us not to become so familiar with the man of God and the Word that we fail to give it (the Word), it's respect. The enemy wants you to take God's word lightly. You must rebuke that spirit and esteem the Word as a vital necessity. And even though you don't worship men and women of God, you still need to keep your distance so you can maintain a level of respect for the word of God that will proceed from their lips. Those who strive to know men and women of God after the flesh limit the anointing.

#12
BRINGS SILENCE

Rejection often brings us to a place where we have nothing or very little to say. Sometimes this is one of the most missed blessings of rejection. It is a time of silence that brings the Father to your defense. As long as you're talking about the rejection and those who did something negative towards you the Lord can't defend you. He will only defend us when we hold our peace. We must remain calm and trust God.

Acts 8:32 *"The place of the scripture which he read was this, He was led as a sheep to the slaughter: and like a lamb dumb before his shearer, so opened he not his mouth."*

Ecclesiastes 3:7 *"...a time to keep silence, and a time to speak"*

Exodus 14:14 *"The Lord shall fight for you, and you shall hold your peace."*

The silence gives you an opportunity to regroup and re-evaluate the situation. It allows you to closely examine what is working and what isn't working. It gives you a chance to be renewed by God. The silence isn't forever it's just for a season. The silence is to give you a chance to challenge yourself and speak to yourself. It is a pondering time and necessary before you make another God ordained move. And no matter what the adversary has tried to do to you, you will make another move after the silence is over!

The silence is to give your spirit and mind a chance to move ahead of your physical body so the devil won't know what hit him when you throw your next blow. The silence is so the Lord can fill your mouth up with words of blessings instead of curses. Satan expects you to walk around speaking death on everything and everybody, but instead, you will speak the blessings of God over people. Even those who rejected you, you will bless.

The silence is a time to look at areas in your life that you haven't paid close attention to as you ought. While you are doing this, God will show you His might and power in the fight. You will be amazed how much God can get accomplished as you are in a period of silence. It is your dying time and I've never heard a dead man speak.

You've poured out your soul to others and now it's your time to be replenished. The silence is to be seen as precious and well needed to come forth as gold. The silence causes you to become more alert to sounds, noises, and voices. It is like a blind man who allows his other senses to be heightened because he can't see. His ears hear things that the person who can see will miss. The silence is allowing you to hear things you would miss if you were talking. The rejection caused your mouth to close, but it is good, because you can now discern what others can't. The things you discern during this season are going to take you places in God that will blow your mind. Because your mouth is closed for this season, you will hear and see things relating to a brand new season in your life. The silence takes your spirit on a journey to places beyond human intelligence. The silence offers you a larger scope of the plan of God in your life. It is at this time, that your spirit beats up on demons and tells hell you have what it takes to win and the keys to get the job done. As you sit and close your eyes in a silent and alone place you will begin to see stuff turning around. You will begin to see the fulfilled will of God! You will begin to breathe in the breath of God afresh. The silence has helped to transform your life.

The silence gives you a chance to counsel yourself out of the circumstance. Many times we have to speak to our own soul about the dilemma. Anybody who hasn't develop the ability to be their own advisor are not ready to move into the fullness of their destiny.

> Psalms 42:5 *"Why are thou cast down, O my soul? And why art thou disquieted within me? hope in God: for I shall yet praise him, who is the health of my countenance, and my God.*

> The Message Translation says, *"Why are you down in the dumps, dear soul? Why are you crying the blues? Fix my eyes on God—soon I'll be praising again. He puts a smile on my face. He's my God."*

#13
MOVES YOU INTO YOUR GIFT

The Christian walk is indeed a journey with a God who knows everything, but reveals what he knows to you and me in part. This causes our journey with him never to become boring because you are always discovering things about Him, yourself and others. Many of us who are being used by God, can truly say that God knew us better than we knew ourselves. We never knew that God had put certain gifts and talents inside of us that the pain of rejection would bring out.

I can recall being in junior high school trying out for the basketball team. The coach was down to the final cut day and I was hoping to make the team. The day had gone very well for me; however, to my surprise I didn't make the squad. I decided that I was going to ask the coach personally why I didn't make the team. He was my homeroom and history teacher and I knew him well enough to approach him. I also wanted to know in case I decided to try out next year; I could improve on those things he didn't feel I was good at. When we talked he informed me that it was a hard and close decision between releasing me or another young boy. He stated that he decided to just go with the other young boy and hopefully I would try out again next year. I wanted to say, "what kind of stupid decision is this," but I didn't. Instead, I said in my mind, "I will never try out for basketball again; it is a waste of time for me. He may think he will see me next year, but it will never happen." I said to myself like never before, "I'm going to buckle down on the books and succeed another way." I felt if men could just cut you off a team with no real reason why, then that was too much power to give them over my life. This episode of rejection from the team helped me examine how difficult it would be to make it in pro sports, but know that I could control what I did with my mind.

I was always a child who thought a lot. It didn't matter what time of day or night it was. I was always thinking. My mother brought us up in the church so many of my thoughts were about God and eternity. Even before I became a believer in Christ; I remember smoking marijuana with my friends and all of a sudden in their midst I would start talking to them about God. I told them God wasn't pleased with us. I asked them what they thought would happen to us if Jesus came back right now? They responded that I was bringing them down from their high. They stated that one day I was going to be a preacher. I told them they were wrong.

I had no idea that God was showing me the thing he would eventually allow me to do in life. I am totally convinced that we will be pushed into many new avenues as we continue our journey with God. He takes what the enemy means for our destruction and brings out the gift on the inside of us. As we follow Christ, he will use rejection to trigger a passion on the inside of you that can't be quenched. Some people who are cut from a basketball team, return the next year and perform very well. Some become a professional athlete because that is their talent in life. However my gift was to preach deliverance to the captive and introduce them to a God who can do exceeding, abundantly above all we can ask or think.

I can remember my mother, aunts, uncles, and friends while I was sitting around as a child asking me what I was thinking about. I would say, "nothing" and continue to think. I would be asking God why certain things were like they were. I had a drive to win and be victorious at anything I did. I wanted to win even if the game was checkers, chess, old maid or sports. I remember competing in a marble tournament as a kid living in the projects. I had defeated all of my opponents and was down to the last person. I was winning when all of a sudden he grabbed all the marbles out of the ring. He snatched the ones I had lying beside me and ran to present them to the trophy holder. Because so many other young boys were competing, the judges couldn't watch everybody's circle. It was his word against mine. In spite of my persistent complaint as well as my tears, the judge awarded the trophy to him. The reason I mention this story is because it allowed me to know at an early age that truth will not be accepted or believed by every one. Some will reject it and continue to believe the lies being told to them by the devil. Yet it is still our duty to tell them the truth.

These types of situations not only bring out your gift, but challenge you to forgive people. Today this young man and I are good friends and I've played a role in leading his son to Christ.

Proverbs 17:9 *"He that covereth a transgression seeketh love; but he that repeated a matter separateth very friends."*

The Amplified says, *"He who covers and forgives an offense seeks love, but he who repeats or harps on a matter separates close friends."*

Our gift will make room for us and we must remember nobody can try to use another man's gift to get the job done. David couldn't use Saul's armour and spear to slay Goliath. Saul had won many battle's with his armour but none with a sling shot and a stone. It is important that we listen to the Holy Ghost and remain true to our element. It is the only place of His power and grace in our lives.

Proverbs 17:8 *"A gift is as a precious stone in the eyes of him that it: whithersoever it turneth, it prospereth."*

The Message Translation says, *"Receiving a gift is like getting a rare gemstone; any way you look at it, you see beauty refracted."*

God has given you a gift to release and bless the world. Your family, friends, and enemies will be delivered as you diligently work your gift. It has been deposited in your life to bring you into the presence of greatness.

Proverbs 22:29 *"Seest thou a man diligent in his business? He shall stand before kings; he shall not stand before mean men."*

The New Kings James Version (Proverbs 22:29) says, *"Do you see a man who excels in his work? He will stand before kings; He will not stand before unknown men."*

The New Living Translation says, *"Do you see any truly competent workers? They will serve kings rather than working for ordinary people."*

The Message Translation says, *"Observe people who are good at their work-skilled workers are always in demand and admired; they don't take a back seat to anyone."*

#14
MATURES YOU

We are truly in the time of God's glory because of what Jesus Christ has done for us. He tasted death for you and I so we could be brought out of sin into the glory of God. Our Heavenly Father has called us to glory and virtue. However, this doesn't mean that we are exempt from trials, tests or rejection. It just means all of it will be for the glory of God.

II Corinthians 4:15 *"For all things are for your sakes, that the abundant grace through the thanksgiving of many may redound to the glory of God."*

We must trust our God and His word enough not to panic in the midst of storms, persecution or rejection. We must have a hope that goes beyond how things look. Our hope must be strong enough to cause rejoicing to spring forth. The true sign of maturity is how we react to adversity.

Romans 5:2 *"By whom also we have access by faith into this grace wherein we stand, and rejoice in hope of the glory of God."*

The Amplified reads, *"Through Him also we have [our] access (entrance, introduction) by faith into this grace (state of God's favor) in which we [firmly and safely] stand. And let us rejoice and exult in our hope of experiencing and enjoying the glory of God."*

These verses tell us to get excited about the glory! The splendor, honor, and weight of God will be experienced by those who are mature enough to understand that it is not time to faint or lose heart about any aspect of our lives if we are born again. Things are turning toward the glory! Lift up your head and shout unto God with the voice of triumph because of what he is doing on your behalf. We are heirs to the victory of Jesus.

> I Peter 5:10 *"But the God of all grace, who hath called us unto his eternal glory by Christ Jesus, after that ye have suffered a while, make you perfect, stablish, strengthen, settle you."*

> The Message Translation says, *"The suffering won't last forever. It won't be long before this generous God who has great plans for us in Christ—eternal and glorious plans they are!—will have you put together and on your feet for good."*

It is so awesome that God would use a man who had denied the Lord in his early days of walking with Jesus to pen such a profound statement. Peter speaks of a God who will use your suffering to ground you securely. The Peter who writes this has matured. He has walked through certain things to experience the excellence or glory of God.

Athletes understand the grouling process they have to go through in order to stand as a champion at the end of the season. They have to endure off season practice and the preseason games. Also, they have to face different opponents during the regular season and eventually be challenged in the playoffs. They have to defeat the champion from another conference and eventually play in the finals. By this time they are spent to the max. Yet, they must find the resolve to overcome tiredness, wounds, and pressure to be the last team standing. They are finally crowned, but not only are they crowned; some other things have taken place. The team and coaching staff mature together in many areas. They've been given a chance to see how much heart each other has.

They've discovered weaknesses and strengths about themselves that they never knew. They had to put away childish things. They matured enough to focus in on the bigger picture and they have the trophy to prove it. They endured negative press along the way and never allowed their critics to destroy their momentum. They've seen the rewards of their labor.

The body of Christ has to do the same. We must look at the enemies we've had to fight on a daily basis. We must notice how many faith fights we've fought together against the adversary and how much childish stuff we had to put away. The leaders of our day have come to a place of maturity and kept us focus. The bigger picture has caused us to overcome weaknesses and given us a chance to possess the trophy. Nothing the enemy has thrown against us has stopped our momentum. We are a progressive group of called out believers, who believe God more today than we did yesterday. We are ready to take the mountain. The rewards are ours!

> Joshua 14,15 *"As yet I am as strong this day as I was in the day that Moses sent me: as my strength was then, even so is my strength now, for war, both to go out, and to come in. Now therefore give me this mountain..."*

You have matured enough to know that you don't have to put on airs nor try to be somebody you're not. You've accepted God's purposes and plans. You've learned to cast your cares on the Lord and live free from worry.

> I Peter 5:6,7 *"Humble yourselves therefore under the mighty hand of God, that he may exalt you in due time: Casting all your care upon him; for he careth for you."*

The Message Translation says, *"So be content with who you are, and don't put on airs. God's strong hand is on you; he'll promote you at the right time. Live carefree before God; he is most careful with you."*

You should take a good look at where you were at the beginning of the storms and where you are now and see that you've grown. The devil wants you to miss out on how you have matured into the image of Christ. There are things Satan thought you couldn't go through, but you've proved him wrong. You now have more to share with this world as well as with your brothers and sisters in Christ. It is time to move out and do it! You've gone through rejection, but you're not smelling like smoke, neither are your garments destroyed. You're not hurt and the fourth man (Jesus Christ) has shown up. You're a God-made champion. You've been made by the fires of rejection. It didn't kill you. It helped you get to your place called "there." It hasn't been in vain. Your character has been developed. Your mind has been renewed. Those around you will stand amazed as you lift the trophy of God's victory!

CONCLUSION

EATING HEALTHY BEFORE YOU EAT
THE SWEETS

As a child, I was raised by parents who wanted me to eat a balanced meal everyday. Supper was always special because it was balanced with meats, starches, and vegetables. I remember wanting so much to eat some cookies or candy before supper was served, but my parents would always say to my sister, my brother and I, "no sweets until you eat your meal." These words would cause tears to come to our eyes, because sometimes we wanted to eat something while waiting for the supper to finish cooking. Yet, their reply to us was an adamant "no." They weren't being mean, harsh or unfair. They just didn't want the sweets to mess up or spoil our appetite for the healthier food awaiting us. They knew if we would fill our stomachs with cookies and candy; we wouldn't desire any supper. They admonished us to wait and eat the candy or cookies as dessert once we had been eaten the main meal. They wanted us to get something healthy and balanced into our stomachs. They didn't want us to get sick by eating the sweets first.

I believe we have raised up a generation in the kingdom who are trying to eat the sweets first. They need to be admonished by their spiritual parents to save the cookies and candy for later on, after they've eaten their rejections in life. Hopefully, this book has caused you to look at rejection as something that you must eat of in order to be a healthy believer in Christ. I'm trying to tell you don't eat the sweets first or you will get a tummy ache. You will not be a strong healthy believer without this process. No sweets until you've eaten your main course. No unhealthy snacks! It's time to chew on this meat of rejection and let the word of God get into the entire joints and marrow of your bones. Then and only then are you ready for the sweets.

In conclusion, I'll tell you the thing that I've found out. The sweets seem to taste even better once you've eaten the healthier meal. Your house, car, finances, and other temporal things taste even better once you've stood on God's word in the midst of being rejected or some other hardship. So, if you've been rejected get ready to enjoy the sweets!

Printed in the United States
201429BV00002B/193-1023/P

9 781604 774290